HBJ SPELLING

SIGNATURE EDITION

RED

Thorsten Carlson

Richard Madden

HBJ SPELLING

SIGNATURE EDITION

 HARCOURT BRACE JOVANOVICH, PUBLISHERS

Orlando   San Diego   Chicago   Dallas

Acknowledgments

For permission to reprint copyrighted material, grateful acknowledgment is made to the following source:

Harcourt Brace Jovanovich, Inc.: Letter forms from *HBJ Handwriting*. Copyright © 1987 by Harcourt Brace Jovanovich, Inc. Definitions from the *HBJ School Dictionary*. Copyright © 1985, 1977 by Harcourt Brace Jovanovich, Inc.

COVER DESIGN Graphic Concern, Inc.

ART CREDITS

Key: T, Top; B, Bottom; L, Left; C, Center; R, Right.

Michael Adams: 112 (B); Kathy Allert: 156, 157; Cathy Beylon: 147, 187, 188; Wendy Biggins: 78; Janet Bohn: 61, 93, 124; Rick Brown: 175; Suzanne Clee: 11; Olivia Cole: 6, 22, 37(T), 52, 54, 67, 75, 109, 116(T), 130, 132, 151, 179; Roberta Collier: 23, 150, 154; Rick Cooley: 185; Steve Darius: 42(B), 57(B); Diane de Groat: 77, 81; Daniel Del Valle: 13, 128(B), 169(B); Kitty Diamantis: 31, 94, 95; Jill Dubin: 8(T), 9, 43, 80, 89, 99, 118; Tom Dunnington: 12, 186(C); Ethel Gold: 16(B), 42(T & C), 57(Top 3), 66, 104; Carol Inouye: 91, 122; Ann Iosa: 30, 36, 37(B), 140; Susan Jaekel: 83 (T), 163; Rosemary Karen: 87; John Killgrew: 10, 21, 27, 29, 38, 71, 113(B), 128(T), 129, 145, 160, 174, 177(T); Jared Lee: 162; Karen Loccisano: 28, 39, 121, 171(T); Loretta Lustig: 44, 45, 74, 146; Wallop Manyum: 180; Kathleen McCarthy: 25, 101, 138, 139; Jane McCreary: 60; Mike Muir: 173; Sal Murdocca: 4, 24, 43, 76, 79, 102, 111, 117, 152, 178; Susan Nethery: 103, 167; Tom Noonan: 64(B), 116(B); Justin Novak: 47, 105, 161; Sharron O'Neil: 172; Sue Parnell: 8(B), 16(T), 17, 46, 51(T), 59, 63, 64(T), 68(C), 68(B), 83(B), 97, 100, 113(T), 114(T), 120 (TL), 171(B); 184, 186(B); Cathy Pavia: 40, 88, 125, 126; Tom Powers: 34, 56, 114(B); Jan Pyk: 2, 3, 7, 55, 62, 143, 164, 165, 192-216; Dan Siculan: 110, 120; Jerry Smath: 14, 15, 70, 112(T), 131, 144, 166; Suzanne Snider: 92, 158; Barbara Steadman: 181; Pat Stewart: 119, 155; Pat Traub: 68 (T), 170; Gary Undercuffler: 19, 176; Charles Varner: 73; Joe Veno: 26 (B); Justin Wager: 32 (B), 33(L), 85, 86, 106; Nina Winters: 177 (B); Marilou Wise: 142; Jane Yamada: 18, 84, 107, 108; Lane Yerkes: 69, 82, 141, 148, 149, 168, 183; Jerry Zimmerman: 133, 134, 135, 159, 169(T); Tom Vroman: 32(T), 33(R), 63(T), 65(T), 94(T), 125 (T), 156 (T), 187 (T), 189; Bob Shein: P. 1 and Paper Sculpture Pencils throughout.

PHOTO CREDITS

Key: T, Top; B, Bottom; L, Left; C, Center; R, Right.

Cover Photography, Ken Lax; Peter Arnold: 5 (4th), 49, 58 (BR); Click Photos: 5 (B); Bruce Coleman: 5(Top 3), 58(TL), 58(TR), 58(BL), 58(C), 113(L), 146, 175; Ingbert Gruttner: 41, 51, 72, 90, 123; Monkmeyer Press Photos: 98(B); Allan Philiba: 170; Terry Wild: 20, 26(T), 85, 98(T); Woodfin Camp and Assoc.: 137

PRODUCTION AND LAYOUT Tom Vroman Associates

Contents

Study Steps to Learn a Word

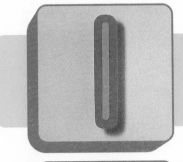 **SAY** the word. Listen to each sound. Think about what the word means.

 **LOOK** at the word. See how the letters are made. Try to see the word in your mind.

 **SPELL** the word to yourself. Think about the way each sound is spelled.

 **WRITE** the word. Copy it from your book. Check the way you made your letters. Write the word again.

 **CHECK** your learning. Cover the word and write it. Did you spell it correctly? If not, do these steps until you know how to spell the word.

Skills Check

A. Write the first letter in the picture name.

1.

2.

3.

4.

B. Write the last letter in the picture name.

5.

6.

7.

8.

C. Write the missing letters in ABC order.

9. b ___ d

10. t ___ v

11. p ___ r

12. g ___ i

D. Write the picture names.

13.

14.

15.

16.

E. Find the word in the box that rhymes with each word. Write the word.

| box | wish | big | fit |

17. hit

18. pig

19. fox

20. fish

F. Find the word in the box that fits each sentence. Add s to the word. Write the word in the sentence.

21. There are oak ____ in the park.

22. Katie likes to play ____.

23. The ____ were barking.

24. Pedro planted the flower ____.

game
seed
tree
dog

best score
D. 4

best score
E. 4

best score
F. 4

total
24

Beginning Sounds

THIS WEEK'S WORDS

1. band
2. bag
3. mad
4. men
5. neat
6. next
7. pan
8. pat
9. real
10. rest

This Week's Words

The first letter in each of these words is a **consonant**. Every letter is a consonant except a, e, i, o, u, and sometimes y.

Point to the consonant at the beginning of each word. Name the letter. Then think of another word you know that starts with that letter.

REMEMBER THIS

The word <u>men</u> means "more than one man."

man

men

Spelling Practice

A. Write two words that begin with the same sound as each picture name. Use This Week's Words.

1.

2.

3.

4.

5.

B. Change the first letter in each word. Write four of This Week's Words.

6. hand

7. can

8. bad

9. nest

Spelling and Language

THIS WEEK'S WORDS

band
bag
mad
men
neat
next
pan
pat
real
rest

Which word fits each sentence? Write the word.

1. Annie met three ___.

mad   men

2. One carried apples in a ___.

band   bag

3. He looked very clean and ___.

neat   next

4. Another carried bread in a ___.

pat   pan

5. He was taller than the ___.

real   rest

Writing on Your Own

Look at the picture on this page. Write two sentences that tell what Annie sees. Use some of This Week's Words in your sentences. Share your sentences with your class.

 WRITER'S GUIDE For help with sentences, turn to page 250.

6

Spelling on Your Own

Look at This Week's Words. Write the word that fits in each shape. Use the letters in the puzzle to help you.

7

be
no
pig
ran

Add a letter to each letter or letters. Write a Mastery word.

1. e **2.** an **3.** o **4.** ig

Follow the directions. Write two Mastery words.

5. Write the word that sounds like 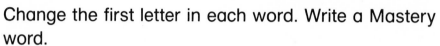 .
6. Write the word that rhymes with ◎ .

Change the first letter in each word. Write a Mastery word.

7. big ___ **8.** can ___

bear
mail
neck
nest
page
robin

BONUS WORDS

Write the Bonus words that end with these letters.

1. st **2.** l **3.** r **4.** ck

Each sentence has one wrong word. Use a Bonus word in place of the wrong word. Write each sentence so that it makes sense.

5. The bear has a nest in the tree.
6. A giraffe has a long page.
7. The baby robin is in the mail.
8. Tracy got a letter in the nest.
9. A neck in this book is torn.
10. My teddy robin lost an ear.

Beginning Sounds

1. tell
2. ten
3. dear
4. does
5. felt
6. fit
7. very
8. went
9. woman
10. your

This Week's Words

Say each word to yourself. Listen carefully to the beginning sound in each word. Point to the letter that stands for the sound. Name the consonant letter that begins each word.

REMEMBER THIS

The word <u>does</u> rhymes with <u>buzz</u> and <u>was</u>. But to spell it, you add <u>es</u> to <u>do</u>. You use <u>does</u> with <u>he</u>, <u>she</u>, and <u>it</u> and with names.

I <u>do</u> my work.
He <u>does</u> his work.
Jenny <u>does</u> her work.

Spelling Practice

A. Each set of letters is in ABC order. But one letter is missing. Write the letter. Then write two of This Week's Words that begin with that letter.

1. a b c __

2. e __ g h

3. r s __ u

4. __ x y z

B. Add the missing letters and write some of This Week's Words.

5. __ __ man

6. __ our

7. __ ery

8. __ oes

C. Finish the second sentence in each pair. Use one of This Week's Words.

9. I have my raincoat.

   Do you have ____ raincoat?

10. Andy likes his dog a lot.

    I like my dog ____ much, too.

10

Spelling and Language

Read the words in each box. Use one to finish each sentence.

1.
| does |
| did |

Tom ___ the dishes every Saturday.

But I ___ them last Saturday.

2.
| told |
| tell |

Grandpa will ___ me a story tonight.

Last night he ___ me one about mice.

3.
| felt |
| feel |

I ___ fine today.

But yesterday I ___ sick.

Writing on Your Own

Write a short letter to a friend. Tell about a trip to the zoo. Use as many of the words in the box as you can.

| tell |
| Dear |
| very |
| went |

 WRITER'S GUIDE If you need help with a letter, turn to page 251.

Spelling on Your Own

tell
ten
dear
does
felt
fit
very
went
woman
your

THIS WEEK'S WORDS

All the letters are consonants except <u>a</u>, <u>e</u>, <u>i</u>, <u>o</u>, and <u>u</u>. These five letters are vowels. The letter <u>y</u> can also be a vowel in some words.

Here are the vowel letters from This Week's Words. Add the consonant letters and write the words. The pictures will help you get started right in **2** and **10**.

1. __ ou __

2. __ e __ __

3. __ o __ a __

4. __ i __

5. __ e __ __

6. __ e __ y

7. __ ea __

8. __ oe __

9. __ e __

10. __ e __ __ .

12

MASTERY WORDS

Write the Mastery word that begins with each of these letters.

1. y

2. f

3. d

4. w

Write the Mastery word that is the opposite of each word.

5. dry

6. no

Write the Mastery word that goes with each word.

7. hands and ___

8. mom and ___

Answer this question. Use two Mastery words.

9. What do boots keep you from getting?

BONUS WORDS

Add these letters and words together to write Bonus words.

1. for + got =

2. to + day =

3. vis + it =

Change a letter in each word to write a Bonus word.

4. hard

5. winner

6. forget

Answer each question with a Bonus word.

7. What do you do with soap and water?

8. What do you do when you go to see someone?

9. What do you call the time between yesterday and tomorrow?

10. What do you call the space behind or in front of a house?

3 Beginning Sounds

THIS WEEK'S WORDS

1. gold
2. gone
3. hall
4. has
5. jar
6. jet
7. left
8. live
9. seed
10. soon

This Week's Words

Say each word to yourself. Listen carefully to the beginning sound in each word. Point to the letter that stands for the sound. Name the consonant letter that begins each word.

REMEMBER THIS

You can say <u>live</u> two ways. You say it both ways in this sentence: "<u>Live</u> animals <u>live</u> in the woods." The first <u>live</u> rhymes with <u>dive</u>. It means that the animals are alive. The second <u>live</u> rhymes with <u>give</u>. It means that the animals make their homes in the woods.

Spelling Practice

A. Follow the directions. Write letters and This Week's Words.

1. Write the first letter in 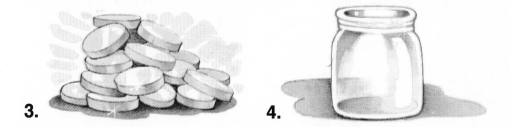. Then write the two words that begin with that letter.

2. Write the first letter in . Then write the two words that begin with that letter.

B. Write the word that goes with each picture. Then write the other word that begins with the same letter.

3.

4.

C. Write the word that has each pair of letters in the middle.

5. oo

6. ee

D. Write a word that rhymes with each word. Use This Week's Words.

7. tall

8. told

9. car

10. give

Spelling and Language

THIS WEEK'S WORDS

gold
gone
hall
has
jar
jet
left
live
seed
soon

Write a sentence with each group of words. Remember two things. A sentence starts with a capital letter. A sentence ends with a period.

1. empty.   jar   The   is

2. the   gone.   jam   All   is

3. plane.   left   Mom   a   in   jet

4. will   soon.   back   She   be

5. Hills   down   The   live   hall.   the

6. Hill   gold   a   has   Al   watch.

Writing on Your Own

Draw a picture of a garden. Then write sentences about your garden. Share your picture and sentences with your class. Use some of This Week's Words in your sentences.

 WRITER'S GUIDE For help with sentences, turn to page 250.

Spelling on Your Own

A. Add a letter to each of these words. This mark ▲ shows where it goes. Write This Week's Words.

1. ▲one
2. ▲all
3. ▲as
4. ▲old
5. see▲
6. son▲
7. lie▲
8. let▲

B. Add <u>p</u> to <u>an</u> and you spell <u>pan</u>. Now follow the directions. Write This Week's Words and other words.

p + an = pan

9. Add <u>g</u>, <u>j</u>, and <u>l</u> to <u>et</u>. Write three words.

10. Add <u>g</u>, <u>h</u>, and <u>c</u> to <u>old</u>. Write three words.

11. Add <u>b</u>, <u>h</u>, and <u>t</u> to <u>all</u>. Write three words.

**he
let
say
see**

Change the first letter in each word. Write a Mastery word.

1. bee   **2.** we

3. way   **4.** met

Finish the sentences. Use the Mastery words.

5. You use your eyes to ____ things.

6. You use your voice to ____ things.

7. Your ears ____ you hear things.

Write the word that can take the place of <u>Ted</u>.

8. Today <u>Ted</u> rode his bike.

**goodness
happy
heard
joke
large
sunny**

BONUS WORDS

1. Add letters to <u>good</u>, <u>sun</u>, and <u>hear</u> to write three Bonus words.

2. Write the word that means "big."

3. Change <u>s</u> to <u>f</u> in <u>sunny</u>. Then write the Bonus word that goes with the new word.

4. Write the two words that end with <u>y</u>. Draw a line under the two letters that come before <u>y</u>.

5. Use each Bonus word in a sentence.

18

4 The Sound /k/

THIS WEEK'S WORDS

1. cat
2. keep
3. duck
4. cow
5. kite
6. sick
7. cup
8. pick
9. cake
10. cook

This Week's Words

Say <u>cat</u>. Listen to the consonant sound that begins <u>cat</u>. Say <u>duck</u>. You hear the same sound at the end of <u>duck</u>. This is the sign for that sound: /k/. All of This Week's Words have the sound /k/.

There are three ways to spell /k/.

- You spell /k/ with **c** in <u>cat.</u>

- You spell /k/ with **k** in <u>keep</u>.

- You spell /k/ with **ck** at the end of <u>duck</u>.

The words <u>cake</u> and <u>cook</u> begin and end with /k/. The first /k/ is spelled with **c**. The second /k/ is spelled with **k**.

Spelling Practice

A. Follow the directions. Use This Week's Words.

1. Write the five words that begin with /k/ spelled <u>c</u>.

2. Write the two words that begin with /k/ spelled <u>k</u>.

3. Write the three words that end with <u>ck</u>.

4. Write the two words that begin and end with /k/.

B. Jake, Pat, and Rick like words that rhyme with their names. Find the words they like. Write them with the right numbers.

5.

6.

7.

Spelling and Language

Add <u>s</u> to <u>cat</u>. You make a word that names more than one.

$$\textbf{cat} \quad + \quad \textbf{s} \quad = \quad \textbf{cats}$$

A. Add <u>s</u> to some of This Week's Words. Write the words that go with the pictures.

1.   **2.**   **3.**

4.   **5.**   **6.**

B. Use two of the words you wrote to finish the sentences.

7. The _____ are making soup.

8. Three blue _____ are caught in the tree.

Writing on Your Own

Write two sentences to a friend. Tell about a trip to a farm. Use the words <u>cows</u> and <u>ducks</u> in your sentences.

 WRITER'S GUIDE How did you end each sentence? If you need help, turn to page 241.

Spelling On Your Own

cat
keep
duck
cow
kite
sick
cup
pick
cake
cook

THIS WEEK'S WORDS

A. Add the letter for /k/ and write each word.

1. __ ake

2. __ ow

3. __ ook

4. __ at

5. __ up

6. __ eep

7. __ ite

B. Look at the words you wrote for **1–5.** Write the letters to finish the rule.

8. ____ stands for /k/ before ____, ____, and ____.

C. Look at the words you wrote for **6** and **7.** Write the letters to finish the rule.

9. ____ stands for /k/ before ____ and ____.

D. Now try this "word math."

10. sit − t + /k/ = ____

11. pin − n + /k/ = ____

12. dug − g + /k/ = ____

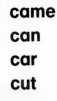

MASTERY WORDS

came
can
car
cut

Which word rhymes with the word in dark print? Write the word.

1. **same**   came   save
2. **but**   bus   cut
3. **far**   car   fat
4. **pan**   can   pat

Which word fits the sentence? Write the word.

5. We rode in the _____.
   car   come

6. Kim _____ out some pictures.
   can   cut

BONUS WORDS

cave
cookie
key
kick
kitten
lucky

Follow the directions. Use the Bonus words.

1. Write the word that rhymes with <u>see</u>. Then write the other words that end with the same sound.
2. Write the word that begins and ends with /k/. How is /k/ spelled at the end? Then write another word that has /k/ spelled the same way.
3. Write the word for a baby cat.

Now try this. Start with the word that rhymes with <u>wave</u>. Follow the directions. Keep writing new words.

4. Change <u>c</u> to <u>g</u>.
5. Change <u>v</u> to <u>m</u>.
6. Change <u>g</u> to <u>n</u>.
7. Change <u>n</u> to <u>c</u>.
8. Change <u>m</u> to <u>v</u> and you are back where you started.

5 Spelling Short <u>a</u>

1. ant
2. past
3. man
4. and
5. as
6. bad
7. fast
8. fat
9. hand
10. last

This Week's Words

The vowel sound in each of the words is called short <u>a</u>. This is the sign for short <u>a</u>: /a/. You spell the sound /a/ with the letter **a.**

24

Spelling Practice

A. Follow the directions. Use This Week's Words.

1. Write the three words that begin with /a/.

2. Write the three words that rhyme.

B. Change the first letter in each word. Write four of This Week's Words.

3. hat

4. band

5. can

6. sad

C. Add <u>s</u> before the <u>t</u> in each word. Write two of This Week's Words.

7. fat

8. pat

D. Finish the poem. Use words that rhyme with the words in dark print.

There once was a huge yellow **cat**
That had grown quite big and __9__ .
Picture, if you **can,**
A cat tall as a __10__
Wearing a coat and a hat.

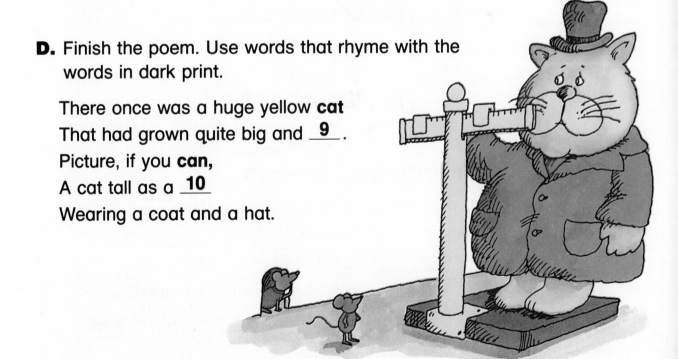

25

Spelling and Language

Here are all the letters in the alphabet in ABC order.

a b c d e f g h i j k l m
n o p q r s t u v w x y z

A. Now write these groups of letters in ABC order.

1. j h g i

2. p r s q

3. b a d f

B. Words can be put in ABC order, too. Write these groups of words in ABC order.

4. fat   bad   and

5. fast   last   hand

Writing on Your Own

Pretend you met a funny ant. Write sentences telling a friend about it. Use some of This Week's Words in your sentences.

WRITER'S GUIDE Did you write neatly? If you need help with any letters, turn to page 257.

WRITER'S GUIDE Did you write neatly? If you need help with any letters, turn to page 257.

THIS WEEK'S WORDS

ant
past
man
and
as
bad
fast
fat
hand
last

Spelling on Your Own

Start with the letter a. Follow the directions. You will write all of This Week's Words.

1. Write the first letter in after a.

2. Write p at the beginning. Write t at the end.

3. Take away p. Use l in its place.

4. Change l to the first letter in .

5. Take away s. Write a word that rhymes with bat.

6. Change f to the first letter in .
   Change t to d.

7. Take away b. Put n in the middle.

8. Write the first letter in at the beginning.

9. Take away d. Change h to m.

10. Take away m. Add the last letter in at the end.

MASTERY WORDS

Follow the directions. Use the Mastery words.

1. Write the two words that rhyme.

2. It begins like <u>h</u>at. It ends like <u>bad</u>. Write the word.

Finish each sentence. Use a Mastery word that begins with the same letter as the name.

3. Serena ___ at the table.

4. Hank ___ a bad cold.

5. I ___ Ann's sister.

6. Andy is ___ the door.

BONUS WORDS

1. Write the two Bonus words that rhyme.
2. Write the three words that begin with two consonant letters.
3. Write the two words that name things to eat.
4. Start with the word <u>ant</u>. Add a letter at the beginning and one at the end. Write a Bonus word.
5. Start with the word <u>and</u>. Add a letter at the beginning and one at the end. Write a Bonus word.
6. Use each Bonus word in a sentence.

Review

Do these steps if you are not sure how to spell a word.

- **Say** the word. Listen to each sound. Think about what the word means.
- **Look** at the word. See how the letters are made. Try to see the word in your mind.
- **Spell** the word to yourself. Think about the way each sound is spelled.
- **Write** the word. Copy it from your book. Check the way you made your letters. Write the word again.
- **Check** your learning. Cover the word and write it. Did you spell it correctly? If not, do these steps until you know how to spell the word.

UNIT 1   **Follow the directions. Use words from Unit 1.**

1. Name the two things in the picture. Write two words with the same beginning sounds.

2. Write the word that begins with the same sound as  .

3. Finish the sentence. Use a word that starts with <u>m</u>.

   The two ___ shook hands.

4. Finish the sentence. Use a word that starts with <u>p</u>.

   Ann put the ___ on the stove.

UNIT 1
bag
next
real
men
pan

29

does
went
woman
your
very

UNIT 2   **Follow the directions. Use words from Unit 2.**

5. Finish the sentence. Write two words that start with <u>w</u>.

The ___ ___ to the store.

6. Write one word to make this sentence a question. <u>Freddie likes to skate</u>.

D ___ Freddie like to skate?

Write the word that begins with the same sound as the picture.

7.

8.

UNIT 3   **Finish each sentence. Use a word from Unit 3. The word should begin with the same sound as the name.**

UNIT 3

gone
left
has
soon
jet

9. Gary is ___ .

10. Luis ___ , too.

11. Heidi ___ to go home.

12. Sue will come ___ .

13. Jim will come on a ___ .

UNIT 4 Add the letters that stand for /k/. Write words from Unit 4.

14. __eep

15. __ook

16. du __

17. coo __

18. __ up

19. pi __

UNIT 4

cook
keep
duck
cup
pick

UNIT 5 Follow the directions. Use words from Unit 5. Write the opposite of each word.

20. slow

21. first

Change the underlined letter in each word. Write a word from Unit 5.

22. band

23. lost

24. sad

25. fan

UNIT 5

bad
last
hand
fast
man

WORDS IN TIME

Some words are very old. Many old words have changed over the years. The word <u>duck</u> started out as the word <u>ducan</u>. <u>Ducan</u> meant **to dive**. People came to use <u>ducan</u> to mean a duck. Why do you think they did that?

31

Spelling and Reading
Sentences That Describe

Read the story. Look for the describing words.

Jamie sat at the table. He ate some carrot cake and drank some milk. His mother called to him. Jamie ran as fast as he could to his mother. He helped her lift a big bag. Then he went back to finish his milk, but it was gone. Where did it go?

Jamie carefully looked around. In a corner, he saw a small, sad cat. It was very thin and the color of gold. It had one blue eye and one yellow eye. Its whiskers were long, white, and dripping with milk.

Jamie smiled. What a surprise! He put some milk in a pan. The cat lapped the milk. Jamie said, "Soon you will be a fat, happy cat!"

Finish each sentence. Use a word from the story.

1. Jamie drank some milk and ate some carrot ＿＿.

2. He helped his mother lift a big ＿＿.

3. He came back and saw a ＿＿.

4. He gave the cat some milk in a ＿＿.

Answer the questions.

5. Do you think Jamie will keep the cat? Why do you think so?

32

Spelling and Writing
Sentences That Describe

Think and Discuss

Look at the picture. Have you seen this cat before? You might know it from the story you read on page 32.

In the story, the writer uses describing words to tell about the cat. What word does the writer use to describe the color of the cat? Is the cat large or small? What shape is the cat? Is it happy or sad at the beginning of the story?

Choose words carefully when you describe something. Use words that tell about size, shape, and color.

Apply

Now it is your turn to write **sentences that describe.** You are going to tell about a make-believe animal. Use words that will help your classmates picture the animal.

Before Writing

Draw a picture of a make-believe animal. We'll call it an Odderbeast.

- Look at your picture. List words that describe the size, shape, and color of your Odderbeast.

Writing

Write some sentences that tell about your Odderbeast.

- Begin with a sentence like this one: <u>I once saw an Odderbeast</u>.
- Write more sentences. Use the words in your list.

After Writing

Read your sentences. Show them to a classmate. Follow these steps to make your sentences better. Use the editing and proofreading marks to show changes.

Editing

- Make sure you used words that tell about size, shape, and color. Add more describing words if you need them.

Proofreading

- Be sure you spelled each word correctly.
- Be sure to begin each sentence with a capital letter. Use a period or question mark at the end of each sentence.

 WRITER'S GUIDE If you need help with capital letters and periods, turn to pages 255 and 256.

Copy your describing sentences onto a clean paper. Write neatly.

Sharing

Share your describing sentences with your classmates. Ask if they can picture your Odderbeast.

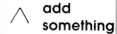 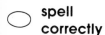

7 Spelling Short e

|e| e

1. pet
2. best
3. dress
4. end
5. help
6. leg
7. sent
8. set
9. well
10. yet

This Week's Words

The vowel sound in each of the words is called short e. This is the sign for short e: /e/. You spell the sound /e/ with the letter **e.**

REMEMBER THIS

The word <u>dress</u>
Ends with double <u>s</u>.
The word <u>well</u>
Ends with double <u>l</u>.

dre**ss**
we**ll**

35

Spelling Practice

pet
best
dress
end
help
leg
sent
set
well
yet

A. Follow the directions. Use This Week's Words.

1. Write the three words that rhyme.

2. Write the four words that end with two different consonant letters.

3. Write the two words that end with two consonant letters that are the same.

B. Read the sentences. They tell you what words to write.

4. You have a foot at the end of it.

5. It is better than <u>good</u> and <u>better</u>.

6. You do this when you give someone a hand.

7. A cat or dog can be one.

8. It is the opposite of <u>beginning</u>.

Spelling and Language

Changing one letter can make a new word. Take <u>ten</u>. Change <u>t</u> to <u>m</u>, and you make <u>men</u>.

Finish these "word ladders." The new letter is already there. Write the rest of the word.

1. nest

   b _ _ _

2. pen

   _ _ t

3. tent

   s _ _ _

4. yes

   _ _ t

5. tell

   w _ _ _

6. red

   b _ _

Writing on Your Own

Look at the picture. Pretend this is your puppy. Write sentences to a pet doctor telling what you think is wrong with it. Use some of This Week's Words in your sentences.

 SPELLING DICTIONARY Do you need help using This Week's Words in sentences? If you do, turn to page 191.

Spelling on Your Own

pet
best
dress
end
help
leg
sent
set
well
yet

Find the word in each row that has the sound /e/. Write the word.

1.	weed	we	well
2.	you	yet	eye
3.	lap	leg	land
4.	pet	pat	pull
5.	sit	sea	set
6.	seat	sent	seed
7.	help	has	heel
8.	ear	eat	end
9.	bat	best	beat
10.	dry	dream	dress

MASTERY WORDS

bed
get
hen
tell

Add the letter that spells /e/. Write the Mastery words.

1. t __ ll
2. g __ t

3. b __ d
4. h __ n

Change the underlined letter in each word. Write a Mastery word.

5. <u>g</u>ot
6. <u>w</u>ell

7. <u>r</u>ed
8. <u>m</u>en

Write a Mastery word to finish each sentence.

9. It is time to ____ up.

10. Jump out of ____, sleepyhead.

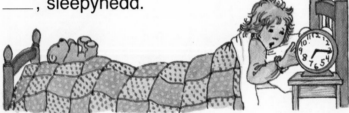

BONUS WORDS

spell
better
spend
desk
step
test

1. Write the three Bonus words that begin with two consonant letters.

2. Write the three words that end with two different consonant letters.

3. Write the two words that have two letters together that are the same.

4. Add a letter right after <u>s</u> to <u>sell</u> and <u>send</u>. Write two Bonus words.

5. Write a short story about school. Use at least four Bonus words.

8 Spelling Short i

1. fill
2. dig
3. fix
4. him
5. his
6. hit
7. if
8. is
9. mix
10. sit

This Week's Words

The vowel sound in each of the words is called short i. This is the sign for short i: /i/. You spell the sound /i/ with the letter **i** in This Week's Words.

40

Spelling Practice

A. Follow the directions. Use This Week's Words.

1. Write the two words that begin with /i/.

2. Write the two words that rhyme with <u>six</u>.

3. Add first letters to <u>it</u>. Write two words.

B. Change the vowel sound in each word to /i/. Write the word.

4. dog

5. fell

6. hum

7. fox

8. set

9. has

10. hat

11. as

C. Write the words that can take the place of <u>Ben</u> and <u>Ben's</u>.

12. I went to the circus with <u>Ben</u>.

13. My dad and <u>Ben's</u> dad went, too.

Spelling and Language

THIS
WEEK'S
WORDS

fill
dig
fix
him
his
hit
if
is
mix
sit

Dig, fill, hit, and sit are "action words," or **verbs**. Sometimes you add s to these words. Then you have verbs to use with names or with he, she, or it. "Gail digs a hole."

Fix and mix are also verbs. You add es to these words. "Eric fixes his bike."

Finish the second sentence in each pair. Remember to add s or es to the verb.

1. I mix red paint with blue paint.

Carlos ____ blue paint with yellow paint.

2. You dig in the garden.

Holly ____ in the garden, too.

3. I fill my glass with milk.

She ____ her glass with apple juice.

4. You sit next to Wendy and me.

Wendy ____ next to you and Chad.

Writing on Your Own

Pretend you fixed this breakfast for someone in your family. Write a short note to put on the tray. Tell the person why you did it. Sign your name. Use some of This Week's Words in your note.

 WRITER'S GUIDE For a sample of a note, turn to page 252.

Spelling on Your Own

What letters do the picture names start with? Write the words that begin and end with these letters.

1.

_ _ _ _

2.

_ _ _

3.

_ _ _

4.

_ _ _

5.

_ _ _ _

6.

_ _ _ _ _ _

7.

_ _ _ _ _

8.

_ _ _ _

9.

_ _ _ _

10.

_ _ _

43

MASTERY WORDS

Change the vowel sound in each word to /i/. Write each word.

1. dad   **2.** on
3. at   **4.** bug

Write a Mastery word that rhymes with each word.

5. dig   **6.** hid

Finish the second sentence with a Mastery word.

7. We will do more work today.

We ___ some work yesterday.

Write this sentence over again. Use a Mastery word in place of <u>His book</u>.

8. <u>His book</u> fell in a big puddle.

BONUS WORDS

The letter <u>C</u> stands for <u>consonant</u>. The letter <u>V</u> stands for <u>vowel</u>. Write the Bonus words that have these letter patterns.

1. CVCC (two words)   **2.** CVCV
3. CCVCC (two words)   **4.** CVCCCV

Follow the directions. Use the Bonus words.
5. Write two words that have the sound /k/.
6. Write the word that has the letter <u>c</u> but not the sound /k/.
7. Write the word that ends like <u>little</u>.
8. Use each Bonus word in a sentence.

Spelling Short u

THIS WEEK'S WORDS

1. jump
2. rub
3. bug
4. just
5. truck
6. luck
7. until
8. come
9. done
10. some

This Week's Words

The vowel sound in each of the words is called short u. This is the sign for short u: /u/. Most of the time, you spell the sound /u/ with the letter **u**. ☐ But in come, done, and some, /u/ is spelled with **o**. Each of these words has an **e** at the end.

REMEMBER THIS

Come, some, done—
It's really sort of fun
To write o-e
And have it be
The vowel sound in run.

Spelling Practice

THIS WEEK'S WORDS

jump
rub
bug
just
truck
luck
until
come
done
some

A. Follow the directions. Use This Week's Words.

1. Write the two words that end with the sound /k/.
2. Write the two words that begin with the letter j.
3. Write the word that begins with /u/.
4. Write the two words that rhyme with <u>hum</u>.
5. Write the word that rhymes with <u>run</u>.

B. Change the vowel sound in each word to /u/. Write the word.

6. rob   7. track

8. beg   9. lick

C. Answer the riddle. Use two words that begin with the same sound as <u>jet</u>.

10. How do cats get on TV?
They ____ ____.

Spelling and Language

Finish the poem with words that rhyme with the words in dark print. Use This Week's Words.

I really **must**
Tell you what __1__
Happened to me.

I saw a **duck**
Driving a __2__,
As plain as can be.

In the back was a **rug.**
On the rug was a __3__,
Big as a bumble bee.

The truck hit a **bump.**
It made the bug __4__
As high as a tree.

Then the truck got **stuck,**
Of all the bad __5__,
Right in front of me.

The duck said, "I **will**
Push hard __6__
The truck is free.

"Would you please **come**
And help us __7__?"
It was pointing at me!

So I did it for **fun,**
Until it was __8__,
THAT is what happened to me!

Writing on Your Own

Find the word in This Week's Words that rhymes with <u>luck</u>. Find the word in This Week's Words that rhymes with <u>some</u>. Write a poem for your classmates with the four words.

 WRITER'S GUIDE For a sample of a poem, turn to page 254.

Spelling on Your Own

jump
rub
bug
just
truck
luck
until
come
done
some

These shapes stand for consonant letters.

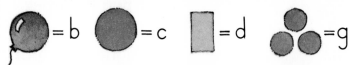

Look at the shapes. Write the letters they stand for. Then add the vowel letters and write This Week's Words.

1.

2.

3.

4.

5.

6.

7.

8.

9.

10.

MASTERY WORDS

fun
up
run
us

Follow the directions. Use the Mastery words.
1. Write the two words that start with /u/.
2. Write the two words that rhyme.
3. What can you do on a hill?
   Write two words.

   I can ___ ___ the hill.

Finish each sentence. Make it mean the same thing as the first sentence. Use a Mastery word.

4. We went higher.
   We went ___ .

5. We had a good time.
   We had ___ .

6. Dad went with Joey and me.
   Dad went with ___ .

BONUS WORDS

funny
month
son
summer
won
wonder

Follow the directions. Use the Bonus words.

1. Four words have /u/ spelled with o. Write these words.
2. Write the words that sound like sun and one. Then use each pair of "sound-alikes" in a sentence.
3. There are twelve of them in a year. May is the name of one of them. Write the word.

Use these clues to find two Bonus Words. Then write each word in a sentence.
4. The first part is fun.
5. The first part sounds like some.

49

THIS WEEK'S WORDS

1. top
2. dog
3. lot
4. job
5. pond
6. pop
7. shop
8. lost
9. soft
10. song

This Week's Words

The vowel sound in <u>top</u> is called short <u>o</u>. This is the sign for short <u>o</u>: /o/. You spell the sound /o/ with the letter **o**.

The word <u>dog</u> has a different vowel sound. Here is the sign for that sound: /ô/. You spell /ô/ with the letter **o,** too.

Spelling Practice

A. Follow the directions. Use This Week's Words.

1. Finish this poem. Write two of This Week's Words.

When Mary Lou sings a ___,

Her ___ tries to sing along.

2. Write the three words that rhyme with <u>hop</u>.

3. Write the four words that end with two consonant letters.

B. Write the word that is the opposite of each word.

4. found

5. hard

6. bottom

C. Finish each sentence. Use a word that rhymes with the name.

7. Bob did a good ___.

8. His friend Scott helped a ___.

51

Spelling and Language

THIS WEEK'S WORDS

top
dog
lot
job
pond
pop
shop
lost
soft
song

Add <u>s</u> to <u>dog</u>. You make a word that names more than one.

 dog + s = dogs

Add <u>s</u> to the word in dark print. Write a word that will finish each sentence.

pond

1. The park has two ____.

dog

2. These ____ all look alike.

song

3. Ann knows many ____.

shop

4. This street has many ____.

Writing on Your Own

Look at the picture. Then write a HELP WANTED sign to put in the shop window. On the sign, tell what the helper's job would be. Use some of This Week's Words in your sentences.

 WORD BOOK If you need more verbs to tell about the helper's job, turn to page 217.

Spelling on Your Own

Use these letters to **begin** the words.

Use these letters to **end** the words.

Find the beginning letter and ending letter that match the color of the number. The red <u>d</u> and the red <u>g</u> go with the red <u>1</u>. Add the letter for /o/ or /ô/ in the middle to finish the word. Write the word next to the number.

1   2   3   4

5   6   7   8

9   10

53

box
got
fox
stop

Add the letter for /o/. Write the Mastery words.

1. st __ p

2. f __ x

3. b __ x

4. g __ t

Follow the directions. Use the Mastery words.

5. Write the two words that rhyme.

6. Write the word that rhymes with <u>hop</u>.

7. Finish the answer to the question. Use a Mastery word. What did you get at the store?

    I ___ milk and bread.

clock
cost
drop
frog
moss
lock

BONUS WORDS

Read these riddles. Answer them with Bonus words.

1. What is green and hops? What is green and doesn't hop?

2. What tells how much it is? What tells how late it is?

3. What means "make it fall"? What means "make it safe from all"?

Try this "word math."

4. clap − p − /a/ + /o/ + /k/ =

5. dry − y + /o/ + pan − an =

6. fry − y + /ô/ + gray − ray =

7. look − ook + /o/ + /k/ =

8. man − n − /a/ + /ô/ + ss =

9. cat − t − /a/ + /ô/ + st =

11 Double Letters

THIS WEEK'S WORDS

1. buzz
2. across
3. ball
4. egg
5. cross
6. fell
7. grass
8. miss
9. off
10. pass

This Week's Words

The letters <u>a</u>, <u>e</u>, <u>i</u>, <u>o</u>, and <u>u</u> are vowels. Sometimes <u>y</u> is also a vowel. All the other letters in the alphabet are consonants.

Each of This Week's Words ends with a consonant sound. The sound is spelled with two letters that are alike. We call these **double consonant letters.**

buzz   ball

egg   miss   off

Spelling Practice

1. Write the word for this shape:

2. Add <u>a</u> to the beginning of the word. Write another word.

3. Write three more words that end with <u>ss</u>.

4. Write the two words that end with <u>ll</u>.

5. Write the three words that have the letter <u>a</u> in the middle.

6. Write the word that has the vowel letter <u>u</u>.

7. Write the two words that have the vowel letter <u>e</u>.

8. Finish the answer to this question.
   Use two of This Week's Words.

   What happened to Humpty Dumpty?

   He ___ ___ the wall.

Spelling and Language

Finish each pair of sentences.

● Make the first sentence tell what is happening now.
  Add <u>es</u> to the word in dark print.

● Make the second sentence tell what already
  happened. Add <u>ed</u> to the word in dark print.

cross

1. Mai ____ the street.

2. Mai ____ the street.

buzz

3. The bug ____ around his head.

4. The bug ____ around his head.

pass

5. The rabbit ____ the turtle.

6. The rabbit ____ the turtle.

Writing on Your Own

Pretend you took this photograph for the Little League Newsletter. Write some sentences to go under the picture. Tell what is happening. Use some verbs from This Week's Words in your sentences.

 WORD BOOK For help finding more verbs, turn to page 217.

Spelling on Your Own

buzz
across
ball
egg
cross
fell
grass
miss
off
pass

Say the name of each animal. What consonant sound does it begin with? Then write all the words that <u>end</u> with that sound.

1. Write two words.

2. Write five words.

3. Write one word.

4. Write one word.

5. Write one word.

58

MASTERY WORDS

Add two letters. Write each Mastery word.

1. we __ __   **2.** fi __ __
3. hi __ __   **4.** li __ __ le

Follow the directions. Use the Mastery words.

5. Write the three words that end with <u>ll</u>.

6. Write the word that means the opposite of <u>big</u>.

7. Add <u>ed</u> to <u>fill</u>. Make a word to finish the sentence.

Nell ___ her glass.

BONUS WORDS

add
butter
penny
rabbit
shell
stuff

Double consonant letters can come at the end of a word or in the middle of a word.

1. Write the three Bonus words that end with double consonant letters.

2. Write the three Bonus words that have double consonant letters in the middle.

Write two Bonus words that have each of these short vowel sounds.

3. /a/   **4.** /e/   **5.** /u/

Write a story about a rabbit. Make believe the rabbit lives as people do. Try to use all the Bonus words.

59

Review

Do these steps if you are not sure how to spell a word.

- **Say** the word. Listen to each sound. Think about what the word means.
- **Look** at the word. See how the letters are made. Try to see the word in your mind.
- **Spell** the word to yourself. Think about the way each sound is spelled.
- **Write** the word. Copy it from your book. Check the way you made your letters. Write the word again.
- **Check** your learning. Cover the word and write it. Did you spell it correctly? If not, do these steps until you know how to spell the word.

UNIT 7

best
help
well
sent
yet

UNIT 7 **Finish the sentences. Use words from Unit 7.**

1. Konoko is my ___ friend.

2. We get along very ___ .

3. She will ___ me when I ask her.

4. Yesterday I ___ her a letter.

5. Konoko has not gotten the letter ___ .

Now go back and circle the letter that spells /e/ in each of your answers.

UNIT 8 Follow the directions. Use words from Unit 8.

6. Write the word that can mean a boy or a man.
7. Change the last letter of the word you wrote and write the new word.
8. Now take off the first letter.
9. Change the last letter.
10. Add <u>s</u> to the beginning of the word, and change the last letter.

Now go back and circle the letter that spells /i/ in each of your answers.

UNIT 9 Follow the directions. Use words from Unit 9.

Add the vowel sound. Then write the words.

11. tr __ ck

12. s __ m __

13. d __ n __

14. j __ st

Finish these sentences.

15. Do not go ____ you have dinner.

16. You have ____ enough time to eat.

Circle the letter that spells /u/ in sentences 15 and 16.

UNIT 10 Add the last two letters to make a word from Unit 10. Then write the word.

UNIT 10

job
lost
song
dog
shop

17. so __ __

18. sh __ __

Now go back and circle the letter that spells /o/ in each answer.

Finish these sentences. Use words from Unit 10.

Bert's __19__ ran out the door. Bert said, ''It could get __20__ . It's my __21__ to go after it.''

UNIT 11

across
off
grass
ball
fell

UNIT 11 Follow the directions. Use words from Unit 11.

22. Write two words to finish this sentence. Circle the double consonant in each answer.

Keep ___ the ___!

Keep
___
the
___!

23. Tell what this player is about to do.

She is about to kick the ___.

24. Tell what happened to this runner.

He ___ ___ the line.

WORDS IN TIME

The word <u>truck</u> comes from the word <u>trochos</u>. <u>Trochos</u> meant **a wheel**. People began to use <u>trochos</u> to mean truck. Can you tell why?

Spelling and Reading
Statements and Questions

Read the story that goes with the picture. Look for statements and questions.

Toby is a guide dog. His job is to help Mara. What does Toby do? He goes with Mara when she shops. He helps Mara across a busy street.

Toby can go with Mara into the store. What does Toby do? He just sits until Mara is ready to go.

What does Mara think about her guide dog? She thinks he is her best friend.

Finish each sentence. Use a word from the story.

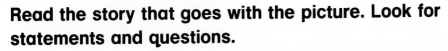

1. Toby is a guide ___ .

2. Toby's job is to ___ Mara.

3. Toby just ___ in the store.

Answer the questions.

4. Why do you think Toby is Mara's best friend?

5. What other things do best friends do?

63

Spelling and Writing
Statements and Questions

**Words to
Help You
Write**

sit
is
some
done
lost
dog
grass
ball

Think and Discuss

You read sentences about Mara and Toby on page 63. Some of the writer's sentences are statements. Some of the sentences are questions.

A statement tells something. It begins with a capital letter. It ends with a period (.).

A question asks something. It begins with a capital letter. It ends with a question mark (**?**).

Read these sentences from the story.

> Toby is a guide dog.
> What does Toby do?

Which sentence is a statement? How can you tell? Which sentence is a question? How can you tell?

Apply

Now it is your turn to write **statements** and **questions**. Write about the picture below. Show your sentences to someone in your family.

Before Writing

Look at the picture on page 64.
What are the cats doing?
- Copy this drawing.
- Add more words that tell what cats do.

 Word Book If you need help finding words, turn to page 217.

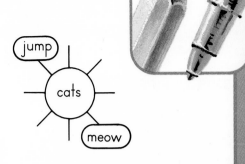

Writing

It is time to write your sentences. Use your drawing.
- Write four statements. Write two questions.
- Make each sentence a complete thought.

After Writing

Read your sentences. Show your sentences to a classmate. Follow these steps to make your sentences better. Use the editing and proofreading marks on this page to show changes you want to make.

Editing

- Make sure you wrote four statements about cats.
- Make sure you asked two questions about cats.

Proofreading

- Be sure you spelled each word correctly.
- Be sure you began each sentence with a capital letter.
- Be sure you ended each statement with a period. Be sure you ended each question with a question mark.

Copy your sentences onto a clean paper. Write neatly.

Sharing

Share your sentences with someone in your family. Ask that person to think up other sentences about cats.

Editing and Proofreading Marks

 capitalize

 make a period

add something

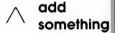 spell correctly

---

65

13 Consonant Clusters

THIS WEEK'S WORDS

1. stand
2. still
3. store
4. glad
5. glass
6. place
7. plant
8. please
9. most
10. must

This Week's Words

Say <u>stand</u> to yourself. Listen to the sounds of the consonant letters <u>s</u> and <u>t</u>.

The letters **st** in <u>stand</u> are called a **consonant cluster.** You write the letters together. You hear the sounds of the letters together.

Most of This Week's Words begin with consonant clusters. The letters **gl** are a cluster. So are the letters **pl.** <u>Most</u> and <u>must</u> end with the cluster **st.**

Spelling Practice

1. Write the word that goes with the picture. Then write two more words that begin with the same cluster.

2. Write the word that names the picture. Then write two more words that have the same cluster.

3. Write the two words that begin with the cluster gl.

4. Write the two words that end with the cluster st.

5. Add es to glass. Name what this boy is wearing.

6. Make the sentence tell about the picture. Begin it with one of This Week's Words. End it with the word you just wrote.

   M__ of these people wear ____.

Spelling and Language

A **noun** is a naming word. A **verb** is an action word. Finish each pair of sentences with the word in dark print. The word will be a verb in the first sentence. It will be a noun in the second sentence.

place
1. I will ___ the plant here.
2. This is a good ___ for it.

store
3. We will ___ the seeds here.
4. Mom bought them at the ___.

stand
5. The plant would not ___ up.
6. We tied the plant to a ___.

Writing on Your Own

Pretend you are going on a trip. You asked a friend to look after your plant. Write a paragraph that explains how to take care of the plant. Use some of This Week's Words.

 **WRITER'S GUIDE** For a sample of a how-to paragraph, turn to page 251.

Spelling on Your Own

THIS WEEK'S WORDS

A. Add the consonant clusters. Write This Week's Words.

1. _ _ ore

2. _ _ ant

3. mu _ _

4. _ _ ill

5. _ _ and

6. mo _ _

7. _ _ ad

8. _ _ ace

B. Write four sentences that ask someone to do something. Begin each sentence with <u>Please</u>. Use the word in dark print in the sentence. Remember that sentences begin with capital letters.

9. store

10. plant

11. glass

12. stand

Please...

play
sleep
story
best

Write the Mastery words that tell what the girl is doing in each picture.

1. _____ **2.** _____

Add pairs of letters and write Mastery words.

3. __ __ ory **4.** be __ __

5. __ __ eep **6.** __ __ ay

Finish the sentence. Write the word that ends with <u>st</u>. Then write the word that begins with <u>st</u>.

7. Becky told the ____ ____ .

stare
steep
stick
dust
trust
playground

Put a consonant cluster in place of the first letter of each word. Write a Bonus word.

1. pick **2.** must **3.** care **4.** deep

Follow the directions. Use the Bonus words.

5. Write the five words that have the cluster <u>st</u>.

6. Write the word that is made up of two words. Draw a line under the consonant cluster that begins each word.

7. Use each Bonus word in a sentence. Try to make your sentences tell a story.

70

14 Consonant Clusters

small

This Week's Words

THIS WEEK'S WORDS

1. small
2. spot
3. swim
4. brother
5. friend
6. from
7. front
8. great
9. pretty
10. true

The letters **sm** in <u>small</u> are a consonant cluster. You write the letters together. You hear the sounds of the letters together.

Each of This Week's Words starts with a consonant cluster. Look at each word. Name the two letters that make up the beginning consonant cluster.

REMEMBER THIS

Here is a sentence to help you remember to put the <u>i</u> before the <u>e</u> in <u>friend</u>. "My <u>friend</u> says <u>I</u> come first."

Spelling Practice

THIS WEEK'S WORDS

small
spot
swim
brother
friend
from
front
great
pretty
true

A. Write words that begin with the same consonant clusters as the words below. Use This Week's Words.

1. brave

2. grow

3. prize

4. tree

B. Follow the directions. Write This Week's Words.

5. Write the three words that begin with <u>fr</u>.

6. Write the three words that begin with <u>s</u> and another consonant letter.

C. Emmy took this picture. Finish the sentences about the picture. Use This Week's Words.

7. This is my best ____, Maria.

8. Maria has a ____ smile.

9. Maria and Julio are ____ and sister.

10. They are standing in ____ of their house.

Spelling and Language

One word is spelled wrong in each sentence. Read the sentence. Find the word that is spelled wrong. Then write the sentence over. Spell all the words the right way.

1. My frend took a trip.

2. I got a postcard form him today.

3. It has a pertty picture on the front.

4. He says they are having a grate time.

Writing on Your Own

Write a postcard to a friend. Tell about a place you have visited or would like to visit. Use some of This Week's Words.

 WORD BOOK Did you use describing words in your postcard? For help finding more describing words, turn to page 217.

Spelling on Your Own

Find each numbered thing in the picture. Say the name of that thing. Then write one of This Week's Words that begins with the same sounds. You will write three words for **8**.

MASTERY WORDS

clean
grass
dress
tree

Read each word. Write the Mastery word that begins with the same two letters.

1. green

2. dry

3. class

4. try

Change the underlined letters. Write two Mastery words.

5. class

6. press

Write one Mastery word to tell about each picture.

7. green ____

8. clean ____

BONUS WORDS

grand
track
smile
bread
sweet
prize

Put a consonant cluster in place of the first letter in each word. Write the Bonus words.

1. hand   **2.** size   **3.** pile

4. back   **5.** feet   **6.** head

Follow the directions. Use the Bonus words.

7. Write two words that start with a consonant cluster made from <u>s</u> and another letter.

8. Write four words that start with a consonant cluster with <u>r</u> in it.

9. Write a word that rhymes with each Bonus word. Then use your word pairs to write a poem.

15 The Letters <u>sh</u> and <u>th</u>

THIS WEEK'S WORDS

1. sheep
2. shoe
3. shut
4. dish
5. finish
6. push
7. wish
8. thank
9. thing
10. teeth

This Week's Words

Say <u>sheep</u>. Listen to the first consonant sound. The two letters **sh** stand for that one sound. The sound is different from the sound that <u>s</u> alone or <u>h</u> alone stands for.

Say <u>teeth</u>. Listen to the last consonant sound. The two letters **th** stand for that one sound. The sound is different from the sound that <u>t</u> alone or <u>h</u> alone stands for.

REMEMBER THIS

Two of This Week's Words name more than one. But neither of them ends with <u>s</u>.

one tooth

many teeth

one sheep

three sheep

Spelling Practice

A. Follow the directions. Use This Week's Words.

1. Write the three words that begin with <u>sh</u>.

2. Write the two words that begin with <u>th</u>.

B. Add two letters that spell one sound. Write the words.

3. fini __ __

4. tee __ __

C. In place of the underlined letter, put two letters that spell one sound. Write some of This Week's Words.

5. <u>d</u>eep

6. di<u>g</u>

7. <u>c</u>ut

8. wi<u>n</u>

9. <u>s</u>ing

10. pu<u>t</u>

D. Add <u>ed</u> to the word in dark print. Write a word to finish each sentence.

11. finish   Pedro ____ making his kite.

12. thank   He ____ his mom for her help.

77

Spelling and Language

THIS
WEEK'S
WORDS

sheep
shoe
shut
dish
finish
push
wish
thank
thing
teeth

You add <u>s</u> to most nouns to make them mean more than one. You add <u>es</u> to nouns that end with <u>sh</u>.

A. Finish each sentence with a noun that means more than one. Add <u>s</u> or <u>es</u> to one of This Week's Words.

1. Jemma made two ____.

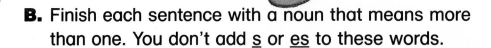

2. One was for red ____.

B. Finish each sentence with a noun that means more than one. You don't add <u>s</u> or <u>es</u> to these words.

3. How many white ____ do you see?

4. The lion has long, sharp ____.

Writing on Your Own

Write a funny story for your friends. Tell about somebody who makes a wish that comes true. Use some of This Week's Words in your story.

 WRITER'S GUIDE For a sample of a story, turn to page 253.

Spelling on Your Own

THIS WEEK'S WORDS

Which words fit together like this? Write the words. Use each of This Week's Words once. Write the number next to each word.

| fish |
| she |
| shop |
| with |

MASTERY WORDS

Follow the directions. Use the Mastery words.

1. Write the two words that start with <u>sh</u>.
2. Write the two words that have short <u>i</u>.

Say each picture name. Listen to the first sound. Then write the Mastery word that ends with that sound.

3.

4.

Write this sentence over. Use a Mastery word in place of <u>Sharon</u>. Begin with a capital letter.

5. Sharon shopped for fish.

| crash |
| earth |
| path |
| shine |
| shout |
| thumb |

BONUS WORDS

1. Write the three Bonus words that begin or end with <u>sh</u>.
2. Write the three words that begin or end with <u>th</u>.
3. Write the two words that name something you can hear.
4. Write the word that rhymes with <u>hum</u>. Then draw a line under the letter that you do not say.
5. Make believe that you just heard a loud crash outside the window. Write a story. Tell what you did when you heard the crash. Tell what made the loud crash. Use as many Bonus words as you can in your story.

80

16 The Letters th and ch

their chair

THIS WEEK'S WORDS

1. their
2. chair
3. than
4. them
5. then
6. these
7. each
8. lunch
9. much
10. watch

This Week's Words

Say <u>their</u>. Listen to the first consonant sound. The two letters **th** stand for that sound.

Say <u>chair</u>. Listen to the beginning sound. Say <u>lunch</u>. Listen to the ending sound. The letters **ch** stand for the sound you hear at the beginning of <u>chair</u> and at the end of <u>lunch</u>.

☐ In <u>watch</u>, the same sound is spelled with three letters: **tch**.

REMEMBER THIS

<u>Their</u> and <u>chair</u> rhyme, but they are not spelled the same. <u>Their</u> begins with the letters that spell <u>the</u>.

their chair

81

Spelling Practice

THIS
WEEK'S
WORDS

their
chair
than
them
then
these
each
lunch
much
watch

A. Follow the directions. Use This Week's Words.

1. Say  . Write the word that has the same first sound.

2. Write the four words that end with the same sound.

3. Write two words that begin the same and end the same.

4. Write three more words that start with <u>th</u>.

B. Write each sentence over. Use one of This Week's Words in place of the underlined words. Remember that sentences start with capital letters.

5. Grandma gave <u>Kevin and Beth</u> new watches.

6. <u>Kevin and Beth's</u> watches are just like mine.

Spelling and Language

Than and then sound almost alike. But they are not the same word at all. Than helps you compare things. "This pencil is longer than that one." Then helps you tell when. "I was only five then."

A. Finish each sentence. Use than or then.

1. Carol is taller ____ Barry.

2. What did you do ____?

3. We played games, and ____ we went home.

4. Nina likes carrots more ____ anything else.

B. Add es to watch. Then use the word twice in one sentence about the picture.

Writing on Your Own

Write a letter to your favorite TV character. Tell why you like his or her show. Use some of This Week's Words.

 WRITER'S GUIDE For help with the parts of a letter, turn to page 251.

Spelling on Your Own

their
chair
than
them
then
these
each
lunch
much
watch

A. Add the letters that spell the missing consonant sound. Write each word.

1. __ air

2. __ en

3. lun __

4. __ eir

5. __ ese

6. wa __

7. ea __

8. __ an

9. mu __

10. __ em

B. Now try this. Start with <u>that</u>. Change one letter at a time. Make a new word to fit each sentence.

that

11. Marco can run faster ____ Todd.

12. They race every now and ____ .

13. Everyone comes to watch ____ .

MASTERY WORDS

Follow the directions. Use the Mastery words.

1. Write the word that goes with the picture.

2. Write the three words that start with <u>th</u>.

3. Write the word that has eight letters but only seven sounds.

Write the words that help tell about the picture.

4. I like ____ dress better than

____ one in the window.

BONUS WORDS

1. Write the three Bonus words that have the last sound heard in <u>each</u>. Underline the letters that spell that sound.

2. Write the three words that have the first sound heard in <u>the</u>.

3. Write a report about the weather where you live. Tell what it is like in the winter and in the summer.

4. Two of the Bonus words rhyme. Write those two words. Then use the words in a two-line poem.

17 Words to Remember

This Week's Words

Read This Week's Words. You know what they mean. You know how to say them. But in some of the words the letters don't stand for the same sounds they stand for in other words. Look at <u>there</u>, <u>here</u>, and <u>were</u>. Each word has the letters <u>ere</u>. Now say <u>there</u>, <u>here</u>, and <u>were</u>. The letters <u>ere</u> stand for different sounds in each word.

Look carefully at each letter in This Week's Words. Try to remember all the letters that make up each word.

REMEMBER THIS

Say <u>there</u>, <u>were</u>, and <u>here</u>.
Each sounds different to the ear.
You must remember what you see
To spell them all with <u>e-r-e</u>.

86

Spelling Practice

A. Follow the directions. Use This Week's Words.

1. Write the three words that end with <u>n</u>.

2. Write the word that ends with <u>ant</u> but doesn't rhyme with  .

3. Write the word that sounds like U U U.

4. Write the four words that end with <u>ere</u>.

5. Draw a line under the two words you wrote for **4** that rhyme with .

6. Circle the word you wrote for **4** that rhymes with .

B. Words with <u>wh</u> begin many questions. Write the word that begins each question. Remember to start with a capital letter.

7. ___ are you going now?

8. ___ will you do?

9. ___ will you get back?

Spelling and Language

THIS WEEK'S WORDS

there
here
were
what
when
where
want
again
been
use

A. Write each group of words in ABC order. Put them in order by first letter.

1. been
   here
   again

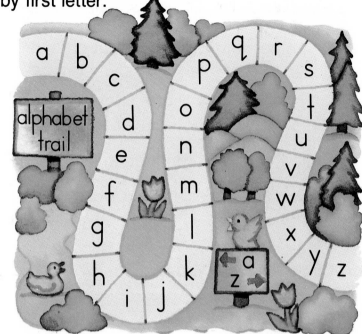

2. use
   there
   what

When words have the same first letter, put them in ABC order by second letter. <u>Wag</u>, <u>wet</u>, and <u>win</u> are in ABC order. They are in order by second letter—<u>a</u>, <u>e</u>, <u>i</u>.

B. Write these groups of words in ABC order. Put them in order by second letter.

3. wind want what   4. where woman were

Writing on Your Own

Draw three pictures that could be added to the Alphabet Trail on this page. Then write three sentences to your teacher telling about your pictures. Use some of This Week's Words in your sentences.

 SPELLING DICTIONARY Do you need help using This Week's Words in sentences? If you do, turn to page 191.

88

Spelling on Your Own

THIS WEEK'S WORDS

A. Read each row of words. Two words rhyme and one does not. Write the word that does not rhyme.

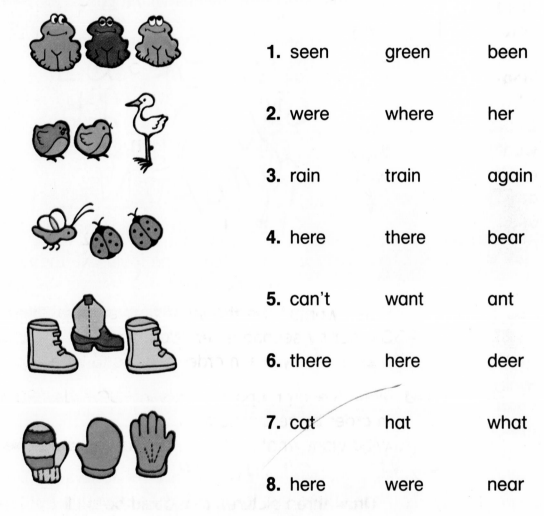

1. seen   green   been

2. were   where   her

3. rain   train   again

4. here   there   bear

5. can't   want   ant

6. there   here   deer

7. cat   hat   what

8. here   were   near

B. Add the vowel letters. Write some of This Week's Words.

9. __ s __

10. __ g __ __ n

11. wh __ n

12. b __ __ n

89

MASTERY WORDS

Follow the directions. Use the Mastery words.

1. Write the word that rhymes with <u>bed</u>.
2. Write the word that rhymes with <u>love</u>.

Read the first sentence in each pair. Then finish the second one. Use a Mastery word.

3. Tammy is seven years old.

   She ____ six last year.

4. I do my best every day.

   Randy ____ his best, too.

5. Lucy says she feels fine today.

   Last night she ____ she felt sick.

wrong
between
listen
family
laugh
thought

BONUS WORDS

1. Write all the Bonus words in ABC order.
2. Write the two words that have the letters <u>gh</u>. Do these letters stand for the same sound in both words?
3. Write the word that has the letter <u>w</u> but no sound for <u>w</u>.
4. Write the word that has the letter <u>t</u> but no sound for <u>t</u>.
5. Draw a picture of someone laughing. Then write a story that tells why the person is laughing. Use as many Bonus words as you can in your story.

90

Review

Do these steps if you are not sure how to spell a word.

- **Say** the word. Listen to each sound. Think about what the word means.
- **Look** at the word. See how the letters are made. Try to see the word in your mind.
- **Spell** the word to yourself. Think about the way each sound is spelled.
- **Write** the word. Copy it from your book. Check the way you made your letters. Write the word again.
- **Check** your learning. Cover the word and write it. Did you spell it correctly? If not, do these steps until you know how to spell the word.

UNIT 13 Follow the directions. Use words from Unit 13. Write the word that rhymes with each of these words.

1. hand
2. just
3. mad
4. more

Circle the consonant clusters in each of your answers. Read this sentence. Then add the word that makes it polite.

5. Close the window, _____ .

UNIT 13
please
stand
must
store
glad

WORDS IN TIME

The word <u>glad</u> comes from the old word <u>glat</u>. <u>Glat</u> was a word that meant **shining.** Think how people look when they are glad. Why did people begin to use <u>glat</u> to mean <u>glad</u>?

UNIT 14

brother
friend
swim
great
true

UNIT 15

shoe
thing
wish
thank
finish

UNIT 14 Add the consonant clusters. Write words from Unit 14.

6. __ __ iend

7. __ __ other

8. __ __ ue

Finish each sentence. Use words from Unit 14.

9. Jeremy can ___ underwater.

10. He says it is ___ fun.

UNIT 15 Follow the directions. Use words from Unit 15.

Say each picture name. Listen to the first sound. Then write the word or words that begin with that sound.

11.

12.

Now go back and circle the letters that make the beginning sound in each word.

Name the picture. Listen to the sound at the end. Then write the two words that end with that sound.

13.

Circle the letters that make the ending sound in each word.

UNIT 16 Follow the directions. Use words from Unit 16.

UNIT 16

chair
watch
their
these
much

14. Write the word for 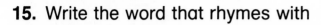 .

15. Write the word that rhymes with 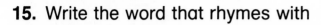 .

16. Write two words that end with the sound you hear at the end of 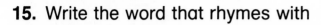 .

Finish the rhyme.

Amy loves to hang in trees.
She says "__17__ trees are great for knees."

UNIT 17 Follow the directions. Use words from Unit 17. Finish each sentence.

UNIT 17

again
been
were
there
here

18. We ___ playing in the park.

19. We had ___ there all morning.

20. After lunch, we played ___ .

21. Read the riddle below. Then use the picture to help you answer the question.

From far to near, come if you can,
From where you are to where I am.

What two places does the riddle talk about?

Spelling and Reading

A Friendly Letter

Read the friendly letter. Look for the five parts of a friendly letter.

Heading

Greeting

Body

Closing

Signature

October 17, 19--

Dear Grandma and Grandpa,

Thank you for the great watch you sent. I love it!

My friend Jimmy and I take swimming lessons. Yesterday we swam to the end of the pool and back again. I wish you could have been there! Good-bye for now. Please come here for Thanksgiving.

Love,

Danny

Finish each sentence. Use a word from the letter.

1. Danny thanked his grandparents for the ___ they sent.

2. Danny swims with his ___ Jimmy.

Answer the questions.

3. Do you think Danny is a good swimmer? Why?

4. How do you think Danny's grandparents will feel when they get his letter?

Spelling and Writing
A Friendly Letter

Words to Help You Write

please
must
store
glad
brother
friend
swim
great
thing
wish
thank
finish
watch
their
much
again
been
where
there
here

Think and Discuss

A friendly letter is a letter you write to someone you know. You can tell about things you do.

To whom did Danny write his letter? What did Danny tell his grandparents about?

Look at the five parts of Danny's letter. Where did Danny use capital letters? Where did he use commas?

Apply

Now it is your turn to write a **friendly letter.**

Before Writing

Think of a friend or relative who lives in another town. Write answers to these questions.

- What is the day, month, and year you are writing?
- What is the name of the person to whom you are writing?
- What one thing do you want to tell about yourself?

Writing

Use your notes to write your letter.

- Tell one thing about yourself.

After Writing

Read your letter. Show it to a classmate. Follow these steps to make your letter better. Use the editing and proofreading marks on this page to show changes you want to make.

Editing

- Make sure your letter has five parts.
- Make sure you have told one thing about yourself.

Proofreading

- Check to be sure you spelled each word correctly.
- Be sure to begin each sentence with a capital letter. Use a period or question mark at the end of each sentence.

Copy your letter onto a clean sheet of paper. Write neatly.

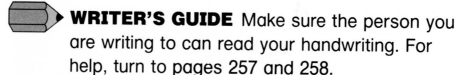 **WRITER'S GUIDE** Make sure the person you are writing to can read your handwriting. For help, turn to pages 257 and 258.

Sharing

If you wish, send your letter. You may want to have someone help you write an envelope.

Editing and Proofreading Marks

≡ capitalize

⊙ make a period

∧ add something

⋏ add a comma

ℓ take something away

◯ spell correctly

19 Spelling Long <u>a</u>

/ā/

a–e

wave

This Week's Words

The vowel sound in most of these words is called long <u>a</u>. This is the sign for long <u>a</u>: /ā/. You spell /ā/ in This Week's Words with **a-consonant-e.**

wave

☐ <u>Have</u> is spelled like a long <u>a</u> word, but it is said with a short <u>a</u>.

REMEMBER THIS

If <u>have</u> doesn't have a long <u>a</u>,
Why is it spelled this way?
Because words seldom end with <u>v</u>.
That's why we add the <u>e</u>.

THIS WEEK'S WORDS

1. wave
2. ate
3. bake
4. face
5. gave
6. late
7. race
8. same
9. save
10. have

Spelling Practice

THIS WEEK'S WORDS
wave
ate
bake
face
gave
late
race
same
save
have

A. Write the two words in each row that rhyme.

1. ate   late   made

2. bake   face   race

3. same   wave   game

4. wave   have   gave

5. make   made   bake

B. Follow the directions. Use This Week's Words.

6. Write the three words that end with <u>ave</u> and have long <u>a</u>.

7. Write the word that ends with <u>ave</u> but doesn't have long <u>a</u>.

C. Read the first sentence. Then finish the others.

Adam has short hair.

8. I ____ long hair.

9. Do you ____ short hair or long hair?

Spelling and Language

Put the letters in front of the word parts to make words.
Write the words in ABC order.

1. | l g |

| ate |

2. | s c |

| ame |

3. | r f |

| ace |

4. | b l |

| ake |

5. | w g |

| ave |

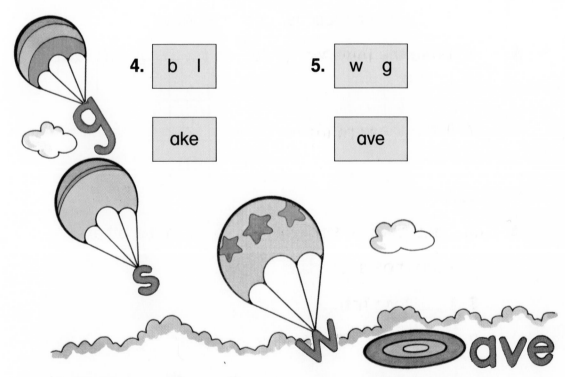

Writing on Your Own

Pretend you went to a friend's party. Write a
thank-you note to your friend. Use some of This
Week's Words.

WRITER'S GUIDE For help with the
parts of a letter, turn to page 251.

Spelling on Your Own

wave
ate
bake
face
gave
late
race
same
save
have

What words fit together like this? Write the words. Use each of This Week's Words once. Write the number for each word.

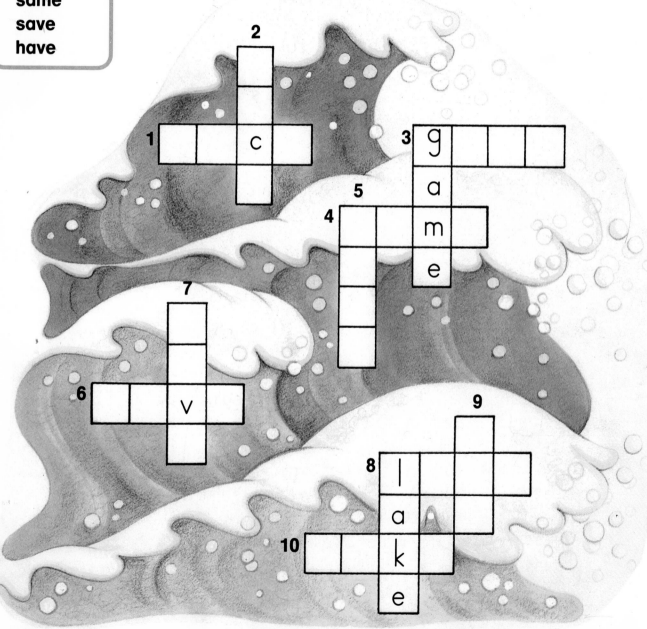

MASTERY WORDS

cake
game
made
make

Say ecch picture name. Write the Mastery word that begins with the same sound.

1.

2.

Follow the directions. Use the Mastery words.

3. Write the two words that are the same except for the first letter.

4. Write the two words that are the same except for the third letter.

Finish the sentences. Use the words that start with <u>m</u>.

5. How many dolls did he ___ ?

6. He ___ five dolls.

BONUS WORDS

brave
lake
safe
shake
skate
snake

1. Look at <u>save</u>. Write a Bonus word that <u>begins</u> with the same two letters. Write one that <u>ends</u> with the same two letters.

2. Look at <u>late</u>. Write a word that <u>begins</u> with the same two letters. Write one that ends with the same two letters.

3. Write the three words that end with the sound /k/. Then write as many words as you can think of that end with <u>ake</u>.

4. Use the Bonus words in sentences. Try to make your sentences tell a story.

20 More Ways to Spell /ā/

1. train
2. nail
3. paint
4. plain
5. tail
6. away
7. may
8. pay
9. stay
10. they

This Week's Words

These words show you more ways to spell /ā/.

● You can spell /ā/ with **ai** in the middle of words.

train

● You spell /ā/ with **ay** at the end of words.

away

☐ Look at <u>they</u>. What letters spell /ā/ in <u>they</u>?

REMEMBER THIS

<u>They</u>, <u>there</u>, <u>these</u>,
If you please,
Start all three
With <u>t</u>-<u>h</u>-<u>e</u>.

Spelling Practice

A. Follow the directions. Use This Week's Words.

1. Write the five words that end with the sound /ā/.

2. Circle the word that is not spelled with <u>ay</u>.

B. Add the letters that spell /ā/. Write the words.

3. p __ __ nt

4. aw __ __

5. th __ __

6. tr __ __ n

7. pl __ __n

8. n __ __ l

C. Write the two words that rhyme with each word.

9. sail

10. rain

D. Which words are spelled wrong? There is one in each sentence. Write it the right way.

11. Thay are painting the house.

12. The dog has paint on its tale.

103

Spelling and Language

THIS
WEEK'S
WORDS

train
nail
paint
plain
tail
away
may
pay
stay
they

You can add ing or ed to verbs, or action words.

A. Add ing to the verb in dark print. Make a word to fit the sentence.

1. **paint**   Nate is ___ a sign.

2. **nail**   Nate is ___ up his sign.

B. Add ed to the verb in dark print. Make the sentence tell what already happened.

3. **stay**   Nate ___ indoors today.

4. **paint**   He ___ a sign.

You do not add ed to pay. You change ay to ai and add d.

C. Finish this sentence. Make it tell what already happened.

5. **pay**   Dad ___ for his work.

Writing on Your Own

Write a paragraph about a game you like to play. Tell what the game is and how you play it. Write the directions to the game in the right order. Share your paragraph with your class.

 WRITER'S GUIDE For a sample of a how-to paragraph, turn to page 251.

Spelling on Your Own

Start with the word <u>way</u>. Do what you are asked to do. You will write all the words.

way

1. Add <u>a</u> at the beginning.

2. Take away <u>aw</u>. Put the first letter in [rat] in its place.

3. Take away <u>p</u>. Put the first letter in [monkey] in its place.

4. Take away <u>m</u>. Put <u>st</u> in its place.

5. Take away <u>s</u> and <u>a</u>. Put <u>h</u> and <u>e</u> between the two letters left.

6. Take away everything but <u>t</u>. After <u>t</u> add the word for [rain cloud] .

7. Take away <u>tr</u>. Put the first two letters in <u>play</u> in its place.

8. Take away <u>l</u>. Put the last letter in [walnut] at the end.

9. Take away <u>p</u> and <u>nt</u>. Put <u>n</u> in front. Put <u>l</u> at the end.

10. Take away <u>n</u>. Put the first letter in [turtle] in its place.

105

rain
wait
day
way

MASTERY WORDS

Follow the directions. Use the Mastery words.
1. Write the two words that end with /ā/.

2. Write the two words that
have /ā/ in the middle.

Finish each sentence.
Use a Mastery word.
3. It is a wet ___ today.

4. I like to play in the
___ .

5. Do you like to play this
___ ?

afraid
trail
clay
maybe
straight
eight

BONUS WORDS

1. Write the Bonus word that means "scared."
2. Write the two words that rhyme. Use both words in
one sentence.
3. Write the word that is made up of two short words.
Use the word in a sentence.
4. Write the word that rhymes with <u>may</u>. Then put
different consonant letters in front of <u>ay</u>. See how
many words you can write.
5. Write the word that rhymes with <u>nail</u>. Then put
different consonant letters in front of <u>ail</u>. See how
many words you can write.

21 Spelling Long <u>e</u>

/ē/

deep

THIS WEEK'S WORDS

1. deep
2. feel
3. free
4. street
5. three
6. mean
7. leave
8. teach
9. many
10. easy

This Week's Words

Each of these words has a vowel sound called long <u>e</u>. This is the sign for long <u>e</u>: /ē/. This Week's Words show three ways to spell /ē/.

● You can spell /ē/ with **ee**.

d**ee**p

● You can spell /ē/ with **ea**.

m**ea**n

● You can spell /ē/ with **y**.

man**y**

107

Spelling Practice

THIS WEEK'S WORDS

deep
feel
free
street
three
mean
leave
teach
many
easy

A. Write a word that rhymes with each word. Use This Week's Words.

1. meet

2. heel

3. keep

B. Add the letters that spell /ē/. Write the words.

4. m __ __ n

5. t __ __ ch

6. l __ __ ve

C. Follow the directions. Use This Week's Words.

7. Write the two words that end with /ē/ spelled **ee**.

8. Write the two words that end with /ē/ spelled **y**.

D. Write the words that are the opposite of these words.

9. hard

10. stay

11. few

12. nice

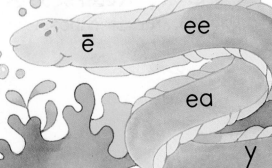

ē   ee

ea

y

Spelling and Language

Some words <u>describe</u>, or tell about, other words. <u>Happy</u> is a describing word. It tells what kind—<u>happy faces</u>. <u>Five</u> is a describing word, too. It tells how many—<u>five fingers</u>.

Read the first sentence in each pair. Then finish the second sentence with a describing word. Use This Week's Words.

1. People kept coming and coming.

There were ___ people at the party.

2. This game is not hard to learn.

It is an ___ game.

3. The water is over Penny's head.

Penny is swimming in ___ water.

4. Erin has two cats and one dog.

Erin has ___ pets.

Writing on Your Own

Look at the picture. Write a paragraph that describes what the boy sees. Tell what he might smell, taste, or touch. Use some of This Week's Words in your paragraph.

 WRITER'S GUIDE For a sample of a paragraph that describes, turn to page 250.

Spelling on Your Own

deep
feel
free
street
three
mean
leave
teach
many
easy

THIS WEEK'S WORDS

Play this word game and write all of This Week's Words. Start with the word you see. Then take letters away or add new ones. When you add /ē/, write one of the three ways to spell this sound.

1. string − ing + /ē/ + t = ___

2. farm − arm + r + /ē/ = ___

3. /ē/ + s + /ē/ = ___

4. tail − ail + /ē/ + ch = ___

5. fit − it + /ē/ + l = ___

6. late − ate + /ē/ + v + e = ___

7. mother − other + an + /ē/ = ___

8. made − ade + /ē/ + n = ___

9. day − ay + /ē/ + p = ___

10. thread − ead + /ē/ = ___

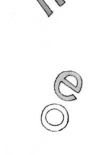

MASTERY WORDS

eat
me
need
we

Follow the directions. Use the Mastery words.

1. Write the two words that end with /ē/. Then write the letter that spells /ē/ in both words.

2. What do you do at breakfast, lunch, and dinner? Write the word.

Change the first letter in each word. Write a Mastery word.

3. he   4. seed

5. be

Write the Mastery words that fit together like this.

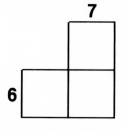

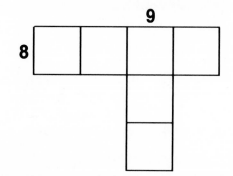

BONUS WORDS

asleep
busy
cheek
dream
empty
treat

Write the Bonus words that mean the opposite of these words.

1. awake   2. full   3. doing nothing

Follow the directions. Write the Bonus words.

4. Write the two words that end with /ē/.
5. Write the word for a part of the face.
6. Write the word for something you like to get.
7. Write a story about a dream. Use all the Bonus words in your story.

111

22 Spelling Long i

THIS WEEK'S WORDS

1. write
2. bike
3. fine
4. fire
5. nice
6. side
7. time
8. tire
9. wide
10. give

This Week's Words

The vowel sound in most of the words is called long i. This is the sign for long i: /ī/. You spell /ī/ in This Week's Words with **i**-consonant-**e**.

write

☐ The word <u>give</u> doesn't have the sound /ī/. But it is spelled with **i**-consonant-**e**.

REMEMBER THIS

Writing <u>write</u> will not trouble you
If you start with a <u>w</u>.

112

Spelling Practice

A. Change the first letter in each word. Write one of
This Week's Words.

1. mine

2. mice

3. like

4. dime

B. Follow the directions. Use This Week's Words.

5. Write the word that goes with the picture.
Then write the word that rhymes with it.

6. Write the word that starts with the first sound
in 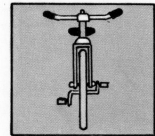 .

7. Draw a line under the first letter in the word you
wrote.

8. Write the word that does not have /ī/.

9. Finish the riddle. Use two words that rhyme with
<u>ride</u>.

It has a pedal on each ____ .

It is not very ____ .

10. Now write the word that answers
the riddle.

Spelling and Language

write
bike
fine
fire
nice
side
time
tire
wide
give

A. Write each group of words in ABC order. Put them in order by first letter.

1. fine
   wide
   side

2. write
   time
   nice

B. Write these groups of words in ABC order. These words have the same first letters. So you must look at the next letter. <u>Cat</u> comes before <u>cut</u> in ABC order. That is because <u>a</u> comes before <u>u</u> in the alphabet.

3. write
   wait
   wide

4. tire
   train
   them

Things to Do
   fix bike
   spend time
   with Jan
   write Grandma

Writing on Your Own

Make up a list of things you need to do at home or at school. Use some of This Week's Words on your list. Put your list where you can see it. Then cross off each thing you do.

 WRITER'S GUIDE For a sample of a list, turn to page 252.

Spelling on Your Own

These shapes stand for consonant letters.

Look at the shapes. Write the letters they stand for.
Then add the vowel letters and write This Week's
Words.

1.  †ire   2. (shapes)

3. (shapes)   4. (shapes)

5. (shapes)   6. (shapes)

7. (shapes)   8. (shapes)

9. (shapes)   10. (shapes)

| **five** |
| **kite** |
| **like** |
| **ride** |

MASTERY WORDS

Follow the directions. Use the Mastery words.

1. Write the two words that have the letter <u>k</u>.

2. Write the word that is a number word.

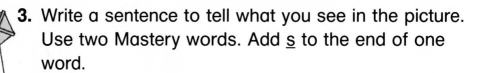

3. Write a sentence to tell what you see in the picture. Use two Mastery words. Add <u>s</u> to the end of one word.

Write the Mastery word that rhymes with each word.

4. bike

5. wide

Finish each sentence. Use the same Mastery word twice.

6. Kelly and Jack went for a ___ .

7. They like to ___ their bikes.

| **hide** |
| **life** |
| **outside** |
| **slide** |
| **twice** |
| **wise** |

BONUS WORDS

Follow the directions. Use the Bonus words.

1. Write the word that is made up of two shorter words.

2. Write the word that means "two times."

3. Write the three words that end with the same three letters. Then use these three words in a sentence.

Write the Bonus word that rhymes with each word.

4. nice   5. prize   6. wife

116

23 More Ways to Spell /ī/

This Week's Words

These words show you four different ways to spell /ī/.

● You can spell /ī/ with **y** at the end of a word after two letters.

sky

● You can spell /ī/ with **i** before **nd**.

find

● You can spell /ī/ with **igh.**

high

● You can spell /ī/ with **ie** at the end of a word after one letter.

tie

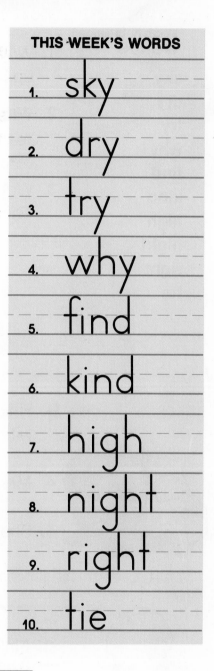

THIS WEEK'S WORDS
1. sky
2. dry
3. try
4. why
5. find
6. kind
7. high
8. night
9. right
10. tie

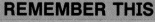
REMEMBER THIS

This ty is too short!

This tie is just right

117

Spelling Practice

THIS
WEEK'S
WORDS

sky
dry
try
why
find
kind
high
night
right
tie

A. Follow the directions. Use This Week's Words.

1. Write the word that sounds like <u>hi</u> and means "far up."

2. Write the five words that rhyme with the word you wrote.

3. Write the word that has just one consonant letter. Then write the letters that spell /ī/ in this word.

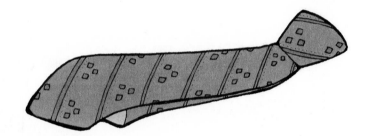

B. Finish the sentences. Use two words that rhyme with <u>mind</u>.

4. Mrs. Jones was very ____ to me.

5. She helped me ____ my lost mitten.

C. Finish the sentences. Use two words that rhyme with <u>light</u>.

6. Last ____ Eric studied for his test.

7. Now he knows his answers will be ____.

Spelling and Language

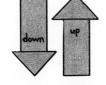

A. Some words mean the opposite of other words. <u>Up</u> and <u>down</u> are opposites. Write a word that means the opposite of each word. Use This Week's Words.

1. lose

2. wrong

3. wet

4. day

5. low

6. mean

B. Write each sentence again. In place of the underlined word, use a word that means the opposite.

7. Angie sleeps all <u>day</u> long.

8. This is the <u>wrong</u> time to sleep.

Writing on Your Own

Write a poem for your teacher. Tell how the sky looks at night. Use the words in the box in your poem.

 WRITER'S GUIDE For a sample of a poem, turn to page 254.

sky
night
find
high

Spelling on Your Own

sky
dry
try
why
find
kind
high
night
right
tie

THIS WEEK'S WORDS

A. Look at each picture. Write the word that goes with the picture. Then write the other words that have /ī/ spelled the same way.

1. Write three words.

2. Write four words.

3. Write two words.

4. Write one word.

B. Now try this. These words have the sound /ē/. Take away the letters that spell /ē/. Add letters that spell /ī/. Write four of This Week's Words.

5. he

6. tree

7. neat

8. tea

MASTERY WORDS

Follow the directions. Use the Mastery words.

1. Write the word that is just one capital letter.

2. Write the other three words in ABC order.

3. Write the word you use to talk about yourself.

4. Write the word that shows something is yours.

Finish the sentences. Use the Mastery words. Use one of them to start every sentence.

5. ___ like ___ new airplane.

6. ___ made it all ___ myself.

7. ___ can make it ___ high.

BONUS WORDS

1. Write the Bonus word that is made up of two shorter words. Then write the other word that has /ī/ spelled the same way.
2. Write the word that means "scare." Then write the other word that has /ī/ spelled the same way.
3. Write the word for a big striped cat. Then write the word for another big cat. What else is alike about these words?
4. Write a story. Make believe you are at the zoo taking pictures. Try to use all the Bonus words in your story.

24 Review

Do these steps if you are not sure how to spell a word.

- **Say** the word. Listen to each sound. Think about what the word means.
- **Look** at the word. See how the letters are made. Try to see the word in your mind.
- **Spell** the word to yourself. Think about the way each sound is spelled.
- **Write** the word. Copy it from your book. Check the way you made your letters. Write the word again.
- **Check** your learning. Cover the word and write it. Did you spell it correctly? If not, do these steps until you know how to spell the word.

UNIT 19

ate
same
have
face
late

UNIT 19 **Follow the directions. Use words from Unit 19. Read the words in the blue box. Write the words in ABC order.**

1. _____

2. _____

3. _____

face
ate
have

Circle the word that does not have /ā/. Finish the sentences.

4. If you are not on time, you are ____ .

5. If you are a twin, you may look the ____ as your brother.

122

UNIT 20 **Add the letters that stand for /ā/. Write the words from Unit 20.**

6. th __ __

7. tr __ __ n

8. aw __ __

9. t __ __ l

10. st __ __

UNIT 20

train
away
they
tail
stay

UNIT 21 **Finish each sentence. Use words from Unit 21. Then circle the letter or letters that spell /ē/.**

11. There are ___ trees on my ___ .

12. It is ___ to pick the apples.

13. Please ___ ___ apples for me.

UNIT 21

three
leave
many
street
easy

UNIT 22 **Follow the directions. Use words from Unit 22. Write the word that goes with each picture.**

14.

15.

16.

Write the word that rhymes with each of these words.

17. tire ___

18. tide ___

UNIT 22

time
write
give
fire
wide

123

UNIT 23 Follow the directions.
Use words from Unit 23.

kind
right
why
sky
night

19. Write the two words that rhyme with <u>light</u>.

20. Write the word that rhymes with <u>mind</u>.

21. Write the words that have /ī/ spelled <u>y</u>.

22. Write the word that sounds like <u>write</u>.

23. Write the word that will make this a rhyming sentence.

Stars at ____ are a lovely sight.

WORDS IN TIME

The word <u>sky</u> comes from an old word that meant **a cloud**. Why do you think people began to use <u>sky</u> to mean **the air above the earth**?

Spelling and Reading
A Story

Read the story. Look for the beginning, middle, and ending.

Once upon a time, there were three neighbors. They lived on the same street in a little town. One neighbor had many tomatoes. One neighbor had a lot of bread. One neighbor had more cheese than she could eat.

The three neighbors talked one day. They were not happy. The first was tired of eating only tomatoes. The second was tired of eating only bread. The third was tired of eating only cheese.

A little boy heard the neighbors talking. A smile crossed his face. He said, ''Your problem is easy to fix. Share your food and make sandwiches!'' The three neighbors thanked the kind boy. Then they all ate sandwiches together.

Finish each sentence. Use a word from the story.

1. This story tells about ____ neighbors.

2. They lived on the same ____ .

3. A little boy said, ''Your problem is ____ to fix.''

Answer the questions.

4. Do you think the neighbors liked the boy? Why or why not?

5. Do you think the boy's idea was a good one? Why or why not?

Spelling and Writing
A Story

Think and Discuss

A story beginning tells about some of the people in the story. Who are the people the writer tells about in the beginning of the story on page 125? A story beginning tells when a story takes place. Where does the writer say the story on page 125 takes place?

The middle of a story is the main part of the story. It tells what the people do. Sometimes it tells about a problem the people have. Why are the three neighbors unhappy in the middle part of the story?

The ending of a story tells how things worked out. It finishes the story. What happens in the ending of the story about the three neighbors?

Apply

Now it is your turn to write a **story.** You can read your story to your classmates.

Before Writing

Think about a story you would like to write. Then write the answers to these questions.

- Who is the story about? Where does the story take place?
- What happens in the story? What do the characters do?
- How does the story end?

Writing

Use your notes and the word list on this page to write your story.

- Write the beginning. Tell who the story is about. Tell where it takes place.
- Write what happens in the middle of your story.
- Write the ending. Tell how everything turns out.

After Writing

Read your story and show it to a classmate. Follow these steps to make your writing better. Use the editing and proofreading marks on this page to show changes you want to make.

 WRITER'S GUIDE For help revising your story, see the checklist on page 248.

Editing

- Make sure your story has a beginning, a middle, and an ending.

Proofreading

- Check to be sure you spelled each word correctly.
- Be sure to begin each sentence with a capital letter.

Copy your sentences onto a clean sheet of paper. Write neatly.

Sharing

Read your story to the class. Ask if anyone can think of another way the story could end.

Editing and Proofreading Marks

	capitalize
	make a period
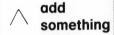	add something
	add a comma
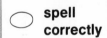	take something away
◯	spell correctly

25 Spelling Long o

THIS WEEK'S WORDS

1. row
2. hope
3. note
4. stone
5. those
6. grow
7. know
8. low
9. slow
10. own

This Week's Words

The vowel sound in each of the words is called long o. This is the sign for long o: /ō/. This Week's Words show two ways to spell /ō/.

● You can spell /ō/ with **o-consonant-e**.

● You can spell /ō/ with **ow**.

REMEMBER THIS

Know sounds like no.
You don't hear the k.
So why take the trouble
To spell it that way?

Just leave off the k,
And you will see how
Without the k
Know becomes now.

Spelling Practice

A. Follow the directions. Use This Week's Words.

1. Write the word that begins with the sound /ō/.

2. Write the five words that end with /ō/.

B. Use the **o**-consonant-**e** way to spell /ō/ in these words. Write the words.

3. st __ n __

4. h __ p __

5. th __ s __

6. n __ t __

C. Follow the directions. Build some of This Week's Words.

7. Add the letters that spell /ō/ after <u>l</u> and <u>r</u>. Write two words.

8. Add a letter to the front of each word you wrote for **7**. You will write two more of This Week's Words.

D. Add a letter to change short <u>o</u> to long <u>o</u>. Write the words.

9. hop

10. not

Spelling and Language

THIS
WEEK'S
WORDS

row
hope
note
stone
those
grow
know
low
slow
own

A. Add <u>s</u> to the verb in dark print. Make a word to fit the first sentence.
Add <u>ing</u> to the verb in dark print. Make a word to fit the second sentence.

1. row   Cindy ____ the boat.

Cindy is ____ the boat.

2. grow   Alan ____ taller every year.

Alan is ____ taller every year.

B. Now add <u>s</u> and <u>ing</u> to <u>hope</u>. You must drop the <u>e</u> before you add <u>ing</u> to <u>hope</u>.

3. hope   Paul ____ to win the race.

Paul is ____ to win the race.

Writing on Your Own

Look at the picture. Pretend you are one of the children. Write sentences telling your teacher how it feels to ride your bike. Use some of This Week's Words in your sentences.

 SPELLING DICTIONARY If you need help using This Week's Words in sentences, turn to page 191.

Spelling on Your Own

THIS WEEK'S WORDS

Follow the directions.
Write This Week's Words.

1. Start with <u>lay</u>.
Change the vowel sound to /ō/.

2. Start with <u>gray</u>.
Change the vowel sound to /ō/.

3. Start with <u>knee</u>.
Change the vowel sound to /ō/.

4. Start with <u>in</u>.
Change the vowel sound to /ō/.

5. Start with <u>hop</u>.
Change the vowel sound to /ō/.

6. Start with <u>not</u>.
Change the vowel sound to /ō/.

7. Start with <u>these</u>.
Change the vowel sound to /ō/.

8. Start with <u>stay</u>.
Add the sound /n/ at the end.
Change the vowel sound to/ō/.

9. Start with <u>run</u>.
Take away <u>n</u>.
Change the vowel sound to /ō/.

10. Start with <u>slid</u>.
Take away <u>d</u>.
Change the vowel sound to /ō/.

MASTERY WORDS

Follow the directions. Write the Mastery words.

1. Write the three words that have /ō/ spelled **o**-consonant-**e**.
2. Write the word that ends with /ō/.

Write the Mastery words that go with these words.

3. jump ___
4. blow your ___
5. come ___
6. ___ and tell

Change the underlined letter in each word to make a Mastery word.

7. <u>h</u>ope
8. ho<u>p</u>e ___

BONUS WORDS

Follow the directions. Use the Bonus words.

1. Write all the words in ABC order. Then draw lines under the letters that spell /ō/.
2. Write the two words that have two vowel sounds.

Write answers to these questions. Use Bonus words.

3. When did you wake up today?
4. Did you speak to Greta yesterday?

Write questions for these answers. Use Bonus words.

5. Yes, I threw the ball that broke the window.
6. The dog followed us all the way home.

132

26 More Ways to Spell /ō/

This Week's Words

Here are three more ways to spell /ō/.

- You can spell /ō/ with <u>o</u> followed by <u>ld</u>.

- You can spell /ō/ with <u>oa</u>.

- You can spell /ō/ with <u>o</u> at the end of a word.

REMEMBER THIS

<u>Also</u> is made up of two words you know: <u>all</u> and <u>so</u>. But one <u>l</u> comes out when you put them together.

THIS WEEK'S WORDS

1. cold
2. toad
3. told
4. ago
5. also
6. goat
7. oak
8. road
9. soap
10. hold

Spelling Practice

THIS
WEEK'S
WORDS

cold
toad
told
ago
also
goat
oak
road
soap
hold

A. Follow the directions. Use This Week's Words.

1. Add different letters in front of old. Write three words.

2. Add letters in front of oad. Write two words.

B. Add the letter or letters that spell /ō/. Write the words.

3. r __ __ d

4. ag __

5. __ __ k

6. s __ __ p

7. als __

8. g __ __ t

C. Finish the story. Use This Week's Words. Use one word twice.

A long time __9__ there was a little brown __10__ that never hopped. No one had ever __11__ this toad that it should hop. One day it snowed. The toad's feet got very __12__. So the toad started to hop to keep its feet out of the snow. Hopping __13__ made the toad feel very warm. The little brown __14__ has been hopping ever since.

Spelling and Language

One word is spelled wrong in each sentence. Read each sentence. Find the word that is spelled wrong. Then write the sentence over. Spell all the words the right way.

1. This is the rode to Joan's house.

2. That oke tree is very old.

3. Roddy tole us a funny joke.

4. Margo allso knows funny jokes.

5. Wash your hands with soup and water.

Writing on Your Own

Look at the picture. Pretend you met this toad on the road. Write sentences that tell what happened. Use some of This Week's Words in your sentences. Proofread your sentences. Make sure all the words are spelled correctly. Read your sentences to the class.

 WRITER'S GUIDE For help revising your sentences, see the editing and proofreading marks on page 249.

Spelling on Your Own

cold
toad
told
ago
also
goat
oak
road
soap
hold

THIS WEEK'S WORDS

Write This Week's Words. The shapes show how many letters each word has. The shapes that are round like the letter <u>o</u> show you where to use letters that spell /ō/. Some of the letters are already there to help.

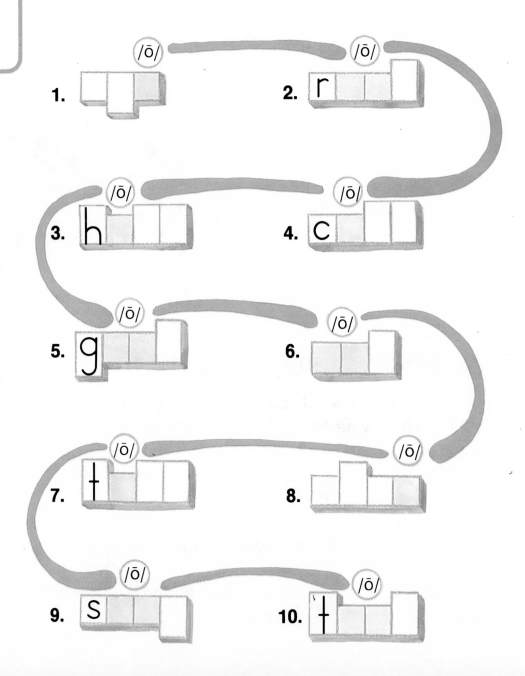

1. /ō/

2. /ō/ r /ō/

3. /ō/ h

4. /ō/ c

5. /ō/ g

6. /ō/

7. /ō/ t

8. /ō/

9. /ō/ s

10. /ō/ t

136

MASTERY WORDS

boat
go
most
so

Follow the directions. Use the Mastery words.

1. Write the two words that rhyme.

2. Write the other word that has /ō/ spelled with <u>o</u>.

3. Change the first letter in <u>coat</u>. Write a Mastery word.

Finish the sentences. Use the Mastery words.

4. The ___ in front is Sandy's.

5. The wind makes it ___ fast.

6. It goes faster than ___ other boats.

BONUS WORDS

both
float
hello
oatmeal
roast
toast

1. Write the Bonus word you can use to talk about two things. Then write the other word that has /ō/ spelled the same way.

2. Write the word that is made up of two shorter words. Then write the other words that have /ō/ spelled the same way.

3. Write the two words that name things you eat for breakfast.

4. Use each Bonus word in a sentence. See if you can make your sentences tell a story.

27 Words with <u>ng</u> and <u>nk</u>

1. long
2. trunk
3. along
4. hang
5. ring
6. sing
7. young
8. bank
9. drink
10. think

This Week's Words

Say <u>long</u>. Listen to the last consonant sound. The two letters **ng** stand for that one sound.

Say <u>trunk</u>. You hear the same sound in <u>trunk</u> just before /k/. The **ng** in <u>long</u> and the **n** in <u>trunk</u> stand for the same sound.

lo**ng**

tru**nk**

REMEMBER THIS

Start <u>young</u> with y-o-u. Think of this sentence. "<u>You</u> are <u>young</u>."

138

Spelling Practice

A. Follow the directions. Use This Week's Words.

1. Write the four words that end with <u>nk</u>.

2. Write the word that means the opposite of <u>short</u>. Then add a letter at the beginning. Write another word.

3. Write four more words that end with <u>ng</u>.

B. Write the verbs, or action words, that go with these words.

4. ___ a song

5. ___ a picture

6. ___ a bell

7. ___ some milk

C. Change the last letter in each word. Write two of This Week's Words.

8. thing ___   **9.** bang ___

Spelling and Language

THIS WEEK'S WORDS

long
trunk
along
hang
ring
sing
young
bank
drink
think

Add <u>s</u> or <u>ing</u> to the verb in dark print so the words will fit the sentences.

1. hang

The monkey ___ upside down.

The monkey is ___ upside down.

2. sing

Susan ___ while she works.

Susan is ___ while she works.

3. drink

Mike ___ a glass of milk.

Mike is ___ a glass of milk.

4. ring

Leon ___ the doorbell.

Leon is ___ the doorbell.

Writing on Your Own

Look at the pictures. Write a story to tell what the girl is doing in each picture. Write a beginning, a middle, and an ending for your story. Share your work with other students.

 WRITER'S GUIDE For a sample of a story, turn to page 253.

Spelling on Your Own

THIS WEEK'S WORDS

A. The letters <u>ng</u> spell one consonant sound. The letters <u>nk</u> spell two consonant sounds. Finish the words. The numbers tell if one or two sounds are missing.

1. si **1**

2. tru **2**

3. you **1**

4. alo **1**

5. dri **2**

6. ha **1**

7. thi **2**

8. ri **1**

9. lo **1**

10. ba **2**

B. Follow the directions. Write This Week's Words and other words.

11. Add <u>s</u>, <u>r</u>, and <u>th</u> to <u>ing</u>. Write three words.

12. Add <u>dr</u>, <u>th</u>, and <u>p</u> to <u>ink</u>. Write three words.

13. Add <u>b</u>, <u>th</u>, and <u>dr</u> to <u>ank</u>. Write three words.

MASTERY WORDS

Follow the directions. Use the Mastery words.

1. Write the two words that end with <u>n</u>.

2. Write the two words that end with <u>n</u> and another letter.

Read the sentence.

A tall man and a short man are going to the fair.

3. Finish this sentence. Make it say about the same thing.

Two ___ are going to the fair.

4. Now make the sentence tell what already happened. Use another Mastery word.

Two men ___ to the fair.

angry
blink
strong
blanket
string
hungry

BONUS WORDS

1. Write the Bonus word that means the opposite of <u>weak</u>. Change the vowel letter to write another Bonus word.

2. Write the Bonus word that means "close both eyes quickly." Change the vowel letter and add two letters at the end. Write another Bonus word.

3. Finish this sentence. Use two words that end with /ē/. The ___ bear looked ___ .

4. Use each Bonus word in a sentence. See if you can make your sentences tell a story.

28 The Sound /o͞o/ in <u>boot</u>

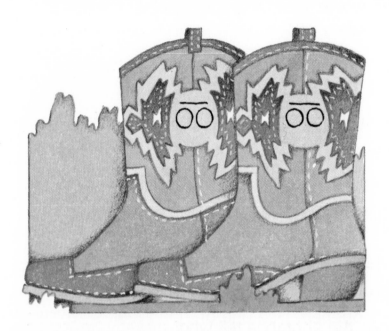

THIS WEEK'S WORDS

1. two
2. new
3. boot
4. to
5. do
6. who
7. too
8. room
9. school
10. blew

This Week's Words

Each of This Week's Words has the same vowel sound. This is the sign for that sound: /o͞o/. The words show three ways to spell /o͞o/.

● You can spell /o͞o/ with one **o**.

tw**o**

● You can spell /o͞o/ with two **o**'s.

b**oo**t

● You can spell /o͞o/ with **ew**.

n**ew**

143

two
new
boot
to
do
who
too
room
school
blew

Spelling Practice

1. Write the two words that have only two letters.

2. Write two words that have /ōō/ spelled the same way.

3. Write the three words that have /ōō/ between consonant sounds.

4. Write the word that is the opposite of <u>old</u>. Then write another word that has /ōō/ spelled the same way.

5. Write the three words that sound alike.

6. Circle the word you just wrote that means "also."

7. Draw a line under the word for <u>2</u>.

8. Finish the second sentence. Make it tell what already happened. Use one of This Week's Words.

   The wind is blowing very hard today.

   The wind ___ hard yesterday, too.

144

Spelling and Language

Finish each sentence with <u>to</u>, <u>too</u>, or <u>two</u>. Remember these things.

- <u>To</u> helps to tell where. It can also come before a verb.
- <u>Too</u> means "also" or "more than enough."
- <u>Two</u> is the word for the number <u>2</u>.

1. Victor went ____ the park.

2. He met ____ friends there, Pam and Eddie.

3. Pam said, "We are going ____ play catch."

4. "You can play, ____," said Eddie.

5. After a while, it started ____ rain.

6. Pam said, "Let's go ____ my house."

Writing on Your Own

Read the sentences on this page again. Then write two or three sentences that tell what Pam, Eddie, and Victor did next. Use some of This Week's Words in your sentences. Read your sentences to a friend.

 WORD BOOK For help finding more verbs, turn to page 217.

Spelling on Your Own

two
new
boot
to
do
who
too
room
school
blew

THIS WEEK'S WORDS

A. Add the letters that spell /o͞o/. Write This Week's Words.

1. sch _ _ l

2. bl _ _

3. r _ _ m

4. d _

5. b _ _ t

6. n _ _

B. Look at the picture. Then finish the sentence that tells what Peter did. Write the sentence with <u>to</u> and <u>two</u> in the right places.

7. Peter brought ___ books ___ school.

8. Now write a sentence that tells what Ned did. Use <u>to</u>, <u>too</u>, and <u>two</u> in your sentence.

C. Now try this "word math."

/o͞o/

9. twice − ice + /o͞o/ = ___

10. why − /ī/ + /o͞o/ = ___

11. blow − /ō/ + /o͞o/ = ___

MASTERY WORDS

soon
shoe
true
you

Follow the directions. Use the Mastery words.

1. Write the word that tells "when." Then write another word that tells "who."

2. Write the word that has /ōō/ spelled <u>ue</u>.

3. Write the word that tells about the picture.

Use Mastery words to finish the poem.

> The sky is green, the grass is **blue.**
> My crayons know just what to **do.**
> Now wait a bit, that can't be ____!
> They almost got mixed up! Did ____?

BONUS WORDS

balloon
broom
flew
grew
raccoon
spoon

Follow the directions. Use the Bonus words.

1. Write the two words that end with /ōō/.
2. Write the two words that have double consonant letters.
3. Write the four words that begin with consonant clusters.
4. Write the two words that name things with handles.

Write the sentences so that they tell what already happened. Use a Bonus word in place of the underlined words.

5. Our baby raccoon <u>is growing</u> up too soon.
6. The red balloon <u>is flying</u> over the roof of the school.

147

29 The Sound /o͝o/ in pull

1. pull
2. full
3. put
4. foot
5. took
6. wood
7. wool
8. could
9. should
10. would

This Week's Words

Each of This Week's Words has the vowel sound you hear in pull. This is the sign for that sound: /o͝o/. The words show three ways to spell /o͝o/.

● You can spell /o͝o/ with **u.**

● You can spell /o͝o/ with **oo.**

● You can spell /o͝o/ with **ou.**

148

Spelling Practice

A. Follow the directions. Use This Week's Words.

1. Write the two words that sound the same.
2. Write three more words that have /o͝o/ spelled as it is in <u>wood</u>.
3. Write two more words that have /o͝o/ spelled as it is in <u>would</u>.

B. Write the words that mean the opposite of these words. Then answer the questions.

4. push   5. empty

6. What letter spells /o͝o/ in these words?

7. What other word has /o͝o/ spelled this way?

C. Finish the sentences. Use the two words that sound alike.

8. Barney ＿＿ like a new doghouse.

9. Let's buy some ＿＿ and build one.

pull
full
put
foot
took
wood
wool
could
should
would

Spelling and Language

THIS WEEK'S WORDS

pull
full
put
foot
took
wood
wool
could
should
would

A. Write each group of words in ABC order. Some of the words begin with the same two letters. So you must look at the third letter.

1. would

took

wood

2. foot

could

full

B. Write the word that fits between these words in ABC order. Use This Week's Words.

5. corner ____ cow

6. puddle ____ push

7. shell ____ shut

8. world ____ wove

Writing on Your Own

Write two sentences to your teacher telling what the picture on this page is about. Use some of This Week's Words in your sentences.

 WRITER'S GUIDE Did you write all your letters neatly so your teacher can read your writing? For help writing letters, turn to pages 257 and 258.

Spelling on Your Own

Read each row of words. Which word rhymes with the word in dark print? Write that word. Remember that words don't have to be spelled the same to rhyme.

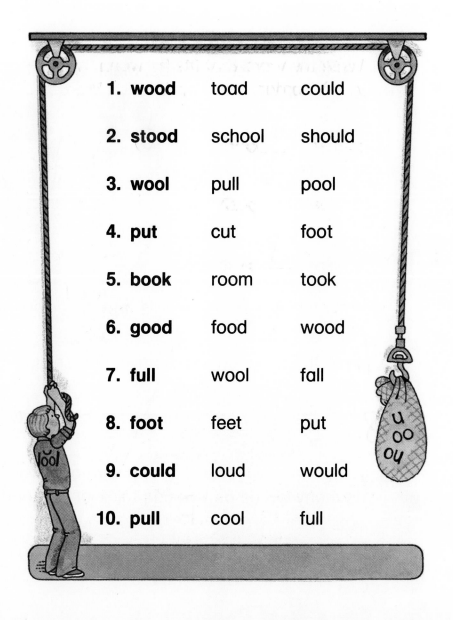

1. **wood**   toad   could

2. **stood**   school   should

3. **wool**   pull   pool

4. **put**   cut   foot

5. **book**   room   took

6. **good**   food   wood

7. **full**   wool   fall

8. **foot**   feet   put

9. **could**   loud   would

10. **pull**   cool   full

151

book
cook
good
look

Follow the directions. Use the Mastery words.

1. Write the three words that rhyme.
2. Write the word that rhymes with <u>wood</u>.

Write the Mastery words that go with these words.

3. ___ at me

4. read a ___

5. ___ news

6. ___ the food

Add <u>ed</u> to two Mastery words. Make words to finish these sentences.

7. Rita ___ dinner.

8. All the food ___ very good.

brook
bulldog
bushes
football
shook
stood

1. Write the four Bonus words that have /o͝o/ spelled as it is in <u>wool</u>.

2. Write the two words that have /o͝o/ spelled as it is in <u>full</u>.

3. Write the two words that are made up of two shorter words.

4. Write the two words that end with <u>ook</u>. Then write as many words as you can think of that end with <u>ook</u>.

5. Write a story about a bulldog. Try to use all the Bonus words in your story.

Do these steps if you are not sure how to spell a word.

- **Say** the word. Listen to each sound. Think about what the word means.
- **Look** at the word. See how the letters are made. Try to see the word in your mind.
- **Spell** the word to yourself. Think about the way each sound is spelled.
- **Write** the word. Copy it from your book. Check the way you made your letters. Write the word again.
- **Check** your learning. Cover the word and write it. Did you spell it correctly? If not, do these steps until you know how to spell the word.

UNIT 25 Follow the directions. Use words from Unit 25.

Write the three words that end with /ō/. Number the words 1–3.

Finish each sentence.

4. She will send a nice ____ to her friends.

5. I like ____ flowers very much.

UNIT 25
grow
know
those
slow
note

WORDS IN TIME

The word <u>note</u> comes from the old word <u>nota</u>. Nota meant **a mark.** Why do you think the word <u>nota</u> became the name for a <u>note</u> you write?

UNIT 26

told
also
soap
cold
road

UNIT 26   **Answer the questions. Use the words from Unit 26.**

6. What do you use to wash behind your ears?

7. What might you get if you forget to wear a coat?

Finish these sentences.

8. We drove down the ____
to pick up Sue.

9. Have I ____ you that Maria is coming,
____?

UNIT 27

along
think
young
sing
drink

UNIT 27   **Finish these sentences. Use words from Unit 27.**

10. Brenda's little brother is very ____.

11. She wants to take him ____ to the park.

12. Do you ____ she should?

13. She will ____ to him and give him
milk to ____.

UNIT 28   Follow the directions. Use words from Unit 28.

Write words that spell /o͞o/ the same way as the words below do.

UNIT 28

who
school
new
do
room

14. too

15. to

16. Finish this sentence.   I wore a ____ dress to the party.

UNIT 29   Follow the directions. Use words from Unit 29.

Read each sentence. Write the word that rhymes with the underlined word.

UNIT 29

took
pull
could
would
put

17. Lois said she <u>would</u> do it tomorrow.

18. She said she <u>could</u> not do it today.

Write the word that rhymes with each of these words.

19. full

20. book

21. Write the word that means the same as <u>set</u>.

Spelling and Reading
Two-Line Rhymes

Read the poem. Listen for the rhyming words.

Tell me where those roses grow.
I would really love to know.

Do they stand in fields of gold?
Do they like the sun or cold?

Could we go there, do you think,
Where crickets sing and bluebirds drink?

Tell me, do you think we could
Go find those flowers in the wood?

Finish each sentence. Use a word from the poem.

1. Tell me where those roses ____.

2. Do roses like the sun or ____?

3. Could we go where crickets ____ and
   bluebirds ____?

Answer the questions.

4. How do you think the writer feels about roses? Why
   do you think as you do?

5. What flowers do you like? Where have you seen
   them growing?

Spelling and Writing
Two-Line Rhymes

Words to Help You Write

grow
know
slow
note
told
cold
road
think
drink
sing
new
do
could
would

Think and Discuss

Words that end with the same sounds are rhyming words. Read these lines from the poem.

Tell me where those roses grow.
I would really like to know.

What two words rhyme? Where is the rhyming word in each line?

Look back at the poem. How many two-line rhymes did the writer write? Name the rhyming words.

Apply

Now it is your turn to write a **two-line rhyme.** You can give your rhyme to a friend on his or her birthday.

Before Writing

- Say the words in the word list on this page.
- Listen for the ending sounds. List words that end with the same sounds.
- Think of other rhyming words. Add them to your list.

Writing

Use your list of rhyming words to write a two-line rhyme.

- Choose two rhyming words.
- Think of something to say using these words.
- Write two rhyming lines.
- If you want to, write two more rhyming lines.

After Writing

Read your poem and show it to a classmate. Follow these steps to make your rhyme better. Use the editing and proofreading marks on this page to show changes you want to make.

Editing

- Make sure your poem has at least two rhyming lines.
- Make sure your lines tell a complete thought.

Proofreading

- Check to be sure you spelled each word correctly.
- Be sure to begin each line with a capital letter.

Copy your lines onto a clean sheet of paper. Write neatly.

WRITER'S GUIDE Make sure the person who reads your poem can read your handwriting. For help writing your letters, turn to pages 257 and 258.

Sharing

Give your poem to a friend on his or her birthday.

Editing and Proofreading Marks

≡	capitalize
⊙	make a period
∧	add something
℮	take something away
⌃,	add a comma
◯	spell correctly
⁋	indent the paragraph

grow
know
slow
throw
go
snow
toe
mow
crow
hoe

31 The Sound /ô/ in <u>paw</u>

THIS WEEK'S WORDS

1. tall
2. call
3. fall
4. wall
5. water
6. paw
7. draw
8. crawl
9. because
10. caught

This Week's Words

Each of This Week's Words has the vowel sound you hear in <u>tall</u>. This is the sign for that sound: /ô/. The words show three ways to spell /ô/.

● You can spell /ô/ with **a**.

t**a**ll

● You can spell /ô/ with **aw**.

p**aw**

● You can spell /ô/ with **au**.

bec**au**se

159

tall
call
fall
wall
water
paw
draw
crawl
because
caught

Spelling Practice

1. Write the four words that end with <u>all</u>.

2. What letter spells /ô/ in these words?

3. Write another word that has /ô/ spelled this way.

4. Write the word that names a dog's foot.

5. What letters spell /ô/ in this word?

6. Write two more words that have /ô/ spelled this way.

7. Write the word you use to tell why.

8. Finish the answer to this question. Use one of This Week's Words.

   Did Amy catch a fish?

   Yes, she ___ a fine fish.

Spelling and Language

This sentence tells you something. "The grass looks brown." This sentence tells why. "It needs water." You can add <u>because</u> to make one long sentence. "The grass looks brown because it needs water."

Put these sentences together with <u>because</u>. Write three long sentences.

1. Everyone clapped.

    Wally caught the ball.

2. Dennis can see the parade.

    He is very tall.

3. The baby crawls.

    He is too young to walk.

Writing on Your Own

Look at the picture of baby Joey. Write a paragraph to your teacher about the picture. Tell why Joey is crawling. Use some of This Week's Words.

 WRITER'S GUIDE For a sample of a paragraph, turn to page 250.

Spelling on Your Own

tall
call
fall
wall
water
paw
draw
crawl
because
caught

One of This Week's Words tells about each picture.
Write the word. Then write all the other words that have
/ô/ spelled the same way.

1. Write five words.

2. Write three words.

3. Write two words.

MASTERY WORDS

Follow the directions. Use the Mastery words.

1. Write the word that means "each and every."

2. Add beginning letters to <u>all</u>. Write two more words.

Finish the sentences. Use two Mastery words that rhyme.

3. Ellie dropped the ____.

4. It rolled down the ____.

Finish both sentences. Use the Mastery word that rhymes with <u>paw</u>.

5. Mr. Ruiz cut the wood with a ____.

6. We ____ him cut it.

BONUS WORDS

always
talk
walk
awful
straw
taught

1. Write the two Bonus words that begin with /ô/.
2. Write the two Bonus words that have an <u>l</u> you don't hear.
3. Write the Bonus word that ends with /ô/.
4. Write this sentence over. Use a Bonus word to tell that this already happened.
> Christy is teaching Glen a new game.
5. Use each Bonus word in a sentence. Try to make your sentences tell a story for a friend to read.

32 The Sound /ou/ in <u>out</u>

THIS WEEK'S WORDS

1. house
2. flower
3. about
4. found
5. our
6. out
7. how
8. now
9. tower
10. town

This Week's Words

Each of This Week's Words has the vowel sound you hear in <u>house</u>. This is the sign for that sound: /ou/. The words show two ways to spell /ou/.

● You can spell /ou/ with **ou**.

● You can spell /ou/ with **ow**.

REMEMBER THIS

Some people say <u>our</u> like <u>are</u>.
"<u>Our</u> friends <u>are</u> on the bus."
Be sure to write <u>o-u-r</u>
When you mean "belonging to us."

164

Spelling Practice

A. Follow the directions. Use This Week's Words.

1. Write the two words that rhyme with the picture name.

2. Write three more words that have /ou/ spelled with <u>ow</u>.

3. Write the word that goes with the picture.

4. Write four more words that have /ou/ spelled with <u>ou</u>.

B. Add <u>s</u> to three of This Week's Words. Write three different words to finish the sentences.

5. Patty and Matt both live in yellow ___.

6. They both have ___ in their yards.

7. But Patty and Matt live in different ___.

house
flower
about
found
our
out
how
now
tower
town

Spelling and Language

<table>
<tr><td>

**THIS
WEEK'S
WORDS**

house
flower
about
found
our
out
how
now
tower
town

</td></tr>
</table>

Finish each poem. Use words that rhyme with the words in dark print. The last word in each poem must rhyme with the last word in the first line. So in the first poem, the last word must rhyme with <u>shout</u>. Use This Week's Words.

The zookeeper heard people **shout**.
He said, "What are they shouting __1__ ?"
So he looked **around**
And then he __2__
That the monkeys had all gotten __3__ .

There once was a king with great **power**
Who lived all alone in a __4__ .
One day he felt **down**.
So he went into __5__
And brought back a big yellow __6__ .

Writing on Your Own

Write two lines that rhyme. Tell about a flower in your poem. Use some of This Week's Words. Read your poem to your class.

WRITER'S GUIDE For a sample of a two-line rhyme, turn to page 253.

166

Spelling on Your Own

THIS WEEK'S WORDS

A. Add the letters that spell /ou/. Write This Week's Words.

1. h __ __ se
2. h __ __
3. f __ __ nd
4. __ __ r
5. t __ __ er
6. n __ __
7. ab __ __ t
8. t __ __ n
9. fl __ __ er
10. __ __ t

B. Now try this "word math."

11. new − /$\overline{oo}$/ + /ou/ = _____
12. to − /$\overline{oo}$/ + /ou/ + er = _____
13. fall − all + /ou/ + nd = _____
14. told − old + /ou/ + n = _____
15. he − /ē/ + /ou/ + se = _____

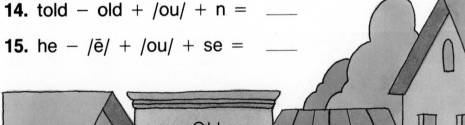

167

boy
cow
down
toy

1. Write the two Mastery words that have /ou/ as in <u>now</u>.

2. Write the two words that do not have the sound /ou/.

3. Put two of the words together. Make a word that goes with the picture.

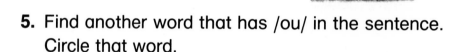

4. Finish the sentence to make it tell about the picture.
   The brown ___ is sitting ___ .

5. Find another word that has /ou/ in the sentence. Circle that word.

clown
ground
mouse
owl
round
sound

BONUS WORDS

1. Write the four Bonus words that have /ou/ spelled <u>ou.</u>
2. Write the two words that have /ou/ spelled <u>ow</u>.
3. Add <u>f</u>, <u>gr</u>, <u>h</u>, <u>r</u>, and <u>s</u> to <u>ound</u>. Write five words.
4. Add <u>br</u>, <u>cl</u>, <u>cr</u>, <u>d</u>, <u>fr</u>, <u>g</u>, and <u>t</u> to <u>own</u>. Write seven words.
5. Mice are afraid of owls. Owls hunt mice for food. Write a different kind of story for someone in your family. Write about a mouse and an owl who are friends. Use as many of the Bonus words as you can.

33 Vowel Sounds with r

This Week's Words

Each of This Week's Words has a vowel sound followed by r. There are two different vowel sounds with r in the words.

You hear one of the vowel sounds with r in part. This is the sign for those sounds: /är/. You spell /är/ with **ar**.

You hear the other vowel sound with r in morning. Here is the sign for those sounds: /ôr/. The words show three ways to spell /ôr/.

● You spell /ôr/ with **or** in torn.
● You spell /ôr/ with **ore** in more.
☐ You spell /ôr/ with **oor** in door.

REMEMBER THIS

There are two o's in door.

169

part
arm
far
hard
start
morning
torn
before
more
door

Spelling Practice

A. Follow the directions. Use This Week's Words.

1. Write the word that goes with the picture.

2. Write four more words that have the sound /ôr/.

3. Write the word that means "not easy" or "not soft."

4. Write four more words that have the sound /är/.

B. Finish each question with the word that means "not the whole thing." Then answer each question with one of This Week's Words.

5. What is a ___ of your body?

6. What is a ___ of the day?

7. What is a ___ of a house?

Spelling and Language

Write each sentence over. In place of the underlined word, write a word that means the opposite. Use This Week's Words.

1. Every <u>evening</u> Gina walks to school.

2. It is a good way to <u>end</u> the day.

3. It is not <u>easy</u> to walk to school.

4. The school is not very <u>close</u>.

5. It is <u>less</u> fun to walk with a friend.

Writing on Your Own

Do you take care of a pet? Do you clean your bedroom? Write a paragraph for a young friend. Tell how you do one home job. Write the steps in the right order. Use some of This Week's Words.

 WRITER'S GUIDE For a sample of a how-to paragraph, turn to page 251.

Spelling on Your Own

part
arm
far
hard
start
morning
torn
before
more
door

THIS WEEK'S WORDS

A. Change the underlined letter in each word to write six of This Week's Words.

1. <u>h</u>orn

2. par<u>k</u>

3. <u>c</u>ard

4. ar<u>t</u>

5. s<u>m</u>art

6. <u>c</u>ar

B. Answer each riddle with one of This Week's Words.

7. Every farmer knows
   This is when a rooster crows.

8. It might have a lock on it.
   If it's closed, you knock on it.

C. Now finish these sentences. Use This Week's Words.

9. Monday comes ___ Tuesday.

10. Ten is two ___ than eight.

11. **G** comes ___ **H** in ABC order.

MASTERY WORDS

are
for
or
jar

Follow the directions. Use the Mastery words.

1. Write the word that sounds like .

2. Take away the <u>f</u>. Write another word.

Write the Mastery word that fits in both sentences.

3. This is a ⎯⎯ of pennies.

4. This is a pickle ⎯⎯ .

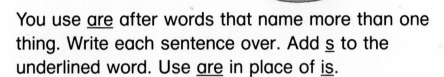

You use <u>are</u> after words that name more than one thing. Write each sentence over. Add <u>s</u> to the underlined word. Use <u>are</u> in place of <u>is</u>.

5. Your <u>sock</u> is on the floor.

6. Your <u>friend</u> is waiting for you.

BONUS WORDS

corner
farm
hardly
order
park
short

1. Write the three Bonus words that have /är/ as in <u>far</u>.

2. Write the three words that have /ôr/ as in <u>morning</u>.

3. Use the Bonus words in sentences that make a story. The story can tell what you like to do in the summer.

Vowel Sounds with <u>r</u>

34

THIS WEEK'S WORDS

1. work
2. bird
3. girl
4. her
5. hurt
6. turn
7. word
8. hear
9. near
10. year

This Week's Words

These words have two more vowel sounds with <u>r</u>. These are the signs for the sounds: /ûr/ and /ir/.

You hear the sounds /ûr/ in <u>work</u>. The words show four ways to spell /ûr/.

● You spell /ûr/ with **er** in <u>her</u>.

● You spell /ûr/ with **ir** in <u>bird</u>.

● You spell /ûr/ with **ur** in <u>hurt</u>.

● You spell /ûr/ with **or** in <u>work</u>.

You hear the sounds /ir/ in <u>hear</u>. You spell /ir/ with **ear** in <u>hear</u>, <u>near</u>, and <u>year</u>.

Spelling Practice

A. Follow the directions. Use This Week's Words.

1. Add letters to the front of <u>ear</u>. Write three words.

2. Write the two words that name things in the picture.

3. Write the two words that begin with the same three letters.

4. Write the two words that have /ûr/ spelled <u>ur</u>.

work
bird
girl
her
hurt
turn
word
hear
near
year

B. Finish the story. Use This Week's Words.

My friend Cara lives __5__ me.
Last __6__ she got a parrot that she named Polly.
The __7__ can talk, but the only __8__ it says
is "Up." When my window is open in
the morning, I __9__ Polly saying,
"Up, up, up!" Cara calls Polly __10__
flying alarm clock.

175

Spelling and Language

**THIS
WEEK'S
WORDS**

work
bird
girl
her
hurt
turn
word
hear
near
year

One word is spelled wrong in each sentence. Read each sentence. Find the word that is spelled wrong. Then write the sentence over. Spell all the words the right way.

1. Meg hurt hur arm.

2. José is a yeer older than Marty.

3. Tern right at the corner.

4. <u>Bird</u> is not a hard wurd to spell.

5. Cover your ears so you will not here.

Writing on Your Own

Look at the picture. Write sentences for your teacher. Tell what is happening in the picture. Use some of This Week's Words.

 WRITER'S GUIDE For help with sentences, turn to page 250.

176

Spelling on Your Own

A. Write the words that fit together like this. Then write the letters that spell /ir/ or /ûr/ in the words.

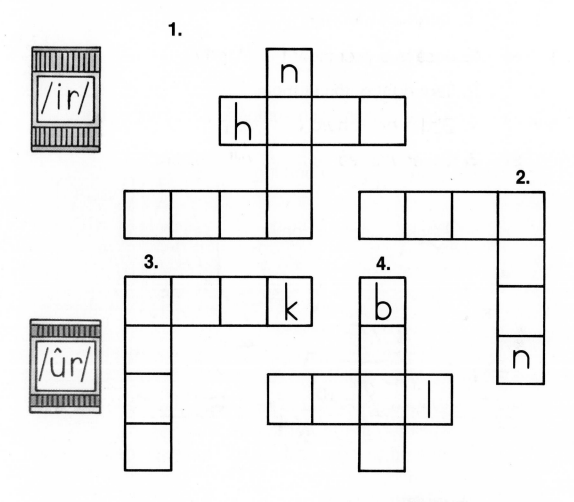

B. Finish these sentences. Use the same word each time.

5. Nancy lost ___ kite.

6. Will you help ___ find it?

dear
here
were
where

MASTERY WORDS

Write the word that rhymes with the word in dark print.

1. **her**   were   where
2. **there**   here   where
3. **near**   bear   here
4. **here**   were   dear

Hear and here sound the same, but they are not spelled the same. Finish each sentence with hear or here.

5. I can ___ a dog barking.

6. Please bring the dog ___ .

early
circus
learn
person
return
world

BONUS WORDS

1. Write each Bonus word. Then write the letters that spell /ûr/ in the word.
2. Add ed to learn and return. Use each new word in a sentence.
3. Write this sentence over. In place of the underlined word, use a Bonus word that means the opposite.

     She got to the party late.

4. Write a story about a person who joins a circus. Try to use all the Bonus words in your story.

178

35 The Sounds /ər/

Here are my father
and sister last winter.

THIS WEEK'S WORDS

1. winter
2. father
3. sister
4. after
5. ever
6. other
7. over
8. color
9. doctor
10. dollar

This Week's Words

Each of This Week's Words ends with a weak vowel sound and <u>r</u>. The weak vowel sound is called **schwa.** This is the sign for schwa: /ə/.

The words show three ways to spell /ər/.

● You spell /ər/ with **er** in <u>winter</u>.

● You spell /ər/ with **or** in <u>color</u>.

● You spell /ər/ with **ar** in <u>dollar</u>.

winter
father
sister
after
ever
other
over
color
doctor
dollar

Spelling Practice

A. Write the word that means the opposite of each word. Use This Week's Words.

1. before

2. under

3. summer

B. Write the words that go with these words. Use This Week's Words.

4. mother and ___

5. nurse and ___

6. brother and ___

C. Here are the first parts of six of This Week's Words. Add the letters that end the words. Write the words.

7. dol _ _ _

8. oth _ _

9. doc _ _ _

10. col _ _

11. af _ _ _

12. ev _ _

D. Answer the riddles. Use This Week's Words.

13. You can spend it, you can save it.
Always thank the one who gave it.

14. When it comes, the wind will blow,
Bringing rain and sometimes snow.

Spelling and Language

Put each group of words in order and write a sentence. Remember two things. A sentence starts with a capital letter. A sentence ends with a period.

1. after   comes   Winter   fall.

2. now.   Winter   over   is

3. father   doctor.   a   Jeff's   is

4. dollar.   My   has   sister   a

Writing on Your Own

Use some of This Week's Words to write a story for someone in your family. Begin your story with the words "Once upon a time." Then write some sentences that tell about the picture on this page. Write a beginning, a middle, and an ending for your story. End your story with the words "They lived happily ever after."

 WRITER'S GUIDE For a sample of a story, turn to page 253.

Spelling on Your Own

winter
father
sister
after
ever
other
over
color
doctor
dollar

A. Here are This Week's Words with stars where the last vowel letters should be. Write the words with the right vowel letters in place of the stars. The first one is done for you.

1. ev★r   ever   **2.** wint★r

3. aft★r   **4.** doll★r

5. col★r   **6.** sist★r

7. ov★r   **8.** doct★r

9. oth★r   **10.** fath★r

B. In the words you wrote, each color star stood for a different vowel letter. Look at the star colors below to check your work.

C. Now that you know what vowel letter each star stands for, use them to write more words.

11. nev★r   **12.** coll★r   **13.** act★r

MASTERY WORDS

brother	
flower	
mother	
water	

Follow the directions. Use the Mastery words.

1. Write the two words that rhyme.

2. Write the name of something that grows in a garden.

3. Write the name of something that all plants need.

Finish the sentences. Make them tell about the pictures.

4. Beth's ___ has a ___ .

5. Beth's ___ is in the ___ .

BONUS WORDS

another
flavor
letter
mirror
sugar
sweater

1. Write these three words: <u>other</u>, <u>color</u>, <u>dollar</u>. Under each word, write the Bonus words that have /ər/ spelled the same way.

2. One of This Week's Words is part of a Bonus word. Write the Bonus word. Write the two words that make it up.

3. Write the two words that have double consonant letters. Then use each word in a sentence.

4. Use each Bonus word in a question. Remember that a question ends with this mark: **?** .

183

Review

Do these steps if you are not sure how to spell a word.

- **Say** the word. Listen to each sound. Think about what the word means.
- **Look** at the word. See how the letters are made. Try to see the word in your mind.
- **Spell** the word to yourself. Think about the way each sound is spelled.
- **Write** the word. Copy it from your book. Check the way you made your letters. Write the word again.
- **Check** your learning. Cover the word and write it. Did you spell it correctly? If not, do these steps until you know how to spell the word.

UNIT 31

water
because
caught
draw
tall

UNIT 31 Follow the directions. Use words from Unit 31.

1–5. Write the words in ABC order.

Now go back and circle the letter or letters in each word that spell /ô/.

UNIT 32 Follow the directions. Use words from Unit 32. Finish the sentences.

UNIT 32

our
about
how
house
now

6. Clare wrote a story ___ a mouse.

Add the letters that stand for /ou/. Write the words.

7. h __ __

8. h __ __ se

9. __ __ r

10. n __ __

UNIT 33 Finish the sentences. Use words from Unit 33.

UNIT 33

part
before
start
door
hard

11. If you don't have all, you may have a ___ .

12. If you want to finish, you have to ___ .

13. If you don't come after, you may come ___ me.

14. If you don't want it closed, you must open the ___ .

15. If your work is not easy, it may be ___ .

Now go back and circle the letters that spell /ôr/ or /är/.

UNIT 34 Follow the directions using words from Unit 34.

UNIT 34

her
girl
year
work
turn

Two words are misspelled in each sentence. Find the words and spell them correctly.

16. A nice gurl moved here last yir.

17. I see hur mom go to wurk every morning.

Finish this sentence.

18. It is Paco's ___ to dry the dishes.

UNIT 35

after
other
color
dollar
over

UNIT 35 Follow the directions using words from Unit 35. Add the letters that spell /ər/. Then write the words.

19. ov _ _

20. col _ _

21. doll _ _

22. aft _ _

23. oth _ _

Finish each sentence.

24. We went to the fair ___ school.

25. I spent a ___ for a balloon.

26. It was hard to choose a ___.

| WORDS IN TIME |

The word <u>dollar</u> comes from the old word <u>Thaler</u>. <u>Thaler</u> meant **silver that was made into coins.** After a time, the letters <u>th</u> changed to <u>d</u>. <u>Thaler</u> became <u>daler</u> and finally <u>dollar</u>.

Spelling and Reading
A How-to Paragraph

Read the how-to paragraph. Look for the way the steps are in order.

Sage and her father are going to build a little house. Sage will play in the house. Before they start, they first draw a plan. Next they get the wood, nails, and tools they will need. Then they choose a spot on which to build. Last they put up the walls and the roof of the house. After the hard part of the work is done, Sage chooses a pretty color for the house. She and her father will paint the house another day.

Finish each sentence. Use a word from the story.

1. This how-to paragraph tells how Sage and her father build a little ____ .

2. First they ____ a plan.

3. Sage chooses a pretty ____ .

Answer the questions.

4. Why do you think Sage and her father wait for another day to paint the house?

5. How do you think Sage felt about helping her father build the playhouse?

187

Spelling and Writing
A How-to Paragraph

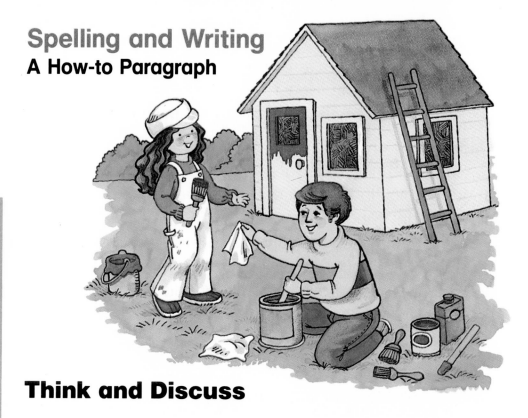

Think and Discuss

A how-to paragraph tells how to make or to do something. What does the writer of the paragraph on page 187 tell you how to do?

A how-to paragraph tells how to do something in order. What does the writer say was the first thing Sage and her father did?

A how-to paragraph uses the words <u>first</u>, <u>next</u>, <u>then</u>, and <u>last</u>. Why did the writer use those words?

Apply

Now it is your turn to write a **how-to paragraph.** You can trade papers with a classmate. Then you can try to follow each other's steps.

Before Writing

Think of some things you know how to make or do.
Here is an example: **How to Make a Greeting Card.**

- Choose something that has only a few steps.
- Make a list of the things needed.
- Make a list of steps to follow.

Writing

Use your lists to write your how-to paragraph.

- Write a sentence that tells what the paragraph is about.
- Write the steps in order.
- Use the words <u>first</u>, <u>next</u>, <u>then</u>, and <u>last</u>.

After Writing

Read your paragraph and show it to a classmate.
Follow these steps to make your work better. Use the
editing and proofreading marks on this page to show
changes you want to make.

 WRITER'S GUIDE For help revising your
paragraph, use the checklist on page 248.

Editing

- Make sure you began with a sentence telling what
  your paragraph is about.
- Make sure the steps are in order.
- Be sure you used the words <u>first</u>, <u>next</u>, <u>then</u>, and <u>last</u>.

Proofreading

- Check to be sure you spelled each word correctly.
- Be sure to begin each sentence with a capital letter.
- Use a period at the end of each statement.

Copy your paragraph onto a clean paper. Write neatly.

Sharing

Share your paragraph with your classmates. Ask them
if they would like to make the thing you tell about.

Editing and Proofreading Marks

≡	capitalize
⊙	make a period
∧	add something
⌄	add a comma
⸋	take something away
◯	spell correctly
⊢	indent the paragraph

SPELLING DICTIONARY

How to Use This Dictionary

The **Spelling Dictionary** can help you understand what words mean. It shows you how to use words in sentences. Sometimes it shows you a picture of the animal or thing the word names.

The words in the dictionary are in ABC order. To find a word you must remember the order of the letters in the alphabet.

A	B	C	D	E	F	G	H	I	J	K	L	M
a	b	c	d	e	f	g	h	i	j	k	l	m

N	O	P	Q	R	S	T	U	V	W	X	Y	Z
n	o	p	q	r	s	t	u	v	w	x	y	z

Suppose you wanted to find <u>wave</u> in the dictionary. First you must find the **W** words. **W** comes near the end of the alphabet, so **W** words will be near the end of the dictionary. The next letter in <u>wave</u> is <u>a</u>. **A** is the first letter of the alphabet, so <u>wave</u> will be near the beginning of the **W** words. Look through the words that begin with <u>wa</u> until you find <u>wave</u>. It is on page 215, between <u>water</u> and <u>way</u>.

about		all

A a

about   Janet collects books <u>about</u> trains. She has <u>about</u> 20 books.

across   We drove <u>across</u> a bridge.

add   Can you <u>add</u> 4 and 11?

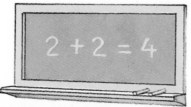

afraid   Billy is not <u>afraid</u> of the dark.

after   You may go <u>after</u> you answer this question. What letter comes <u>after</u> Q?

afternoon   The time between noon and evening. My little sister takes a nap in the <u>afternoon</u>.

again   We read the story in class. Then I read it <u>again</u> at home.

ago   My grandfather was born a long time <u>ago</u>.

all   Louise got 100 on the history test. She answered <u>all</u> the questions correctly.

along

along   We followed the path along the edge of the cliff. My dog came along with us.

also   Brian plays the piano. He also plays the drums.

always   I always brush my teeth after I eat.

am   I am seven years old. I am going on my first plane trip.

and   Tina and Maria are sisters. Tina is six, and Maria is four.

angry   Pat got angry when her brother broke her toy car.

another   May I please have another piece of cake?

ant

anything   You may have anything you want for your birthday.

apple

are   The boys are in the back yard. They are digging a hole.

arm   Amelia's arm is not long enough to scratch her back.

as   The horse was as white as snow.

be

asleep   Kevin was so tired, he fell asleep in the chair.

at   I met Ralph at the zoo. We had fun looking at the animals.

ate   Susan ate a sandwich for lunch. Look at **eat.**

away   Carl went away to camp. He will be away for three weeks.

awful   Our school has a new band. It sounds awful.

B b

bad   If something tastes bad, don't eat it. It may be bad for you.

bag   Ellen carries her lunch in a paper bag.

bake   **baked, baking** We helped bake the cake for the party.

ball   Mike hit the ball over the fence.

balloon

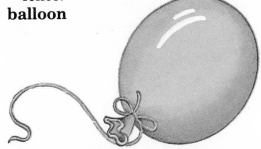

band   Rachel plays a drum in the school band.

bank   Ted put the dimes in his piggy bank. Mrs. Stevens cashed her check at the bank.

be   Please be here on time. I will be waiting for you.

bear		box

bear

because We played in the house <u>because</u> it was raining outside.

bed Adam has a big new <u>bed</u>. He will go to <u>bed</u> early tonight.

been Tony has <u>been</u> late for school every day this week.

before What day comes <u>before</u> Monday? Think <u>before</u> you answer.

best D.J. wore his <u>best</u> suit to his aunt's wedding.

better Al got 80 on the test. Sue got 85. Sue's score was <u>better</u> than Al's.

between The first game was <u>between</u> our school and Central. Melba hit a ball <u>between</u> first and second base.

big Larry lives in a <u>big</u> house with 22 rooms.

bike

bird A bright red <u>bird</u> made a nest in the tree.

black The sky looks <u>black</u> at night.

blanket Rita has a warm <u>blanket</u> on her bed.

blew A strong wind <u>blew</u> from the north. It <u>blew</u> down many trees.

blink Keep your eyes open and don't <u>blink</u>.

blue The sky is blue.

boat

boot

both Carol and Anita are sisters. They <u>both</u> go to our school.

bother Don't <u>bother</u> me when I am studying.

box **boxes** Put all your toys in this <u>box</u>.

boy	**candy**

boy   Three girls and one <u>boy</u> are in the play.

brave   Meg rode the elephant at the zoo. She is a <u>brave</u> girl.

bread

bring   **brought, bringing** What did Chuck <u>bring</u> to the party?

brook   We saw a big fish in the <u>brook</u>.

broom

brother   Ben and his <u>brother</u> both have curly hair.

bug

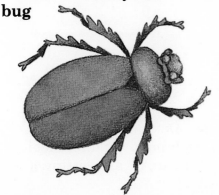

bulldog

bushes   Roses grow on <u>bushes</u>.

busy   Everyone in class was <u>busy</u> planning for the party.

butter   Do you want <u>butter</u> on your toast?

buzz   Bees <u>buzz</u> when they fly.

by   These sand hills were built <u>by</u> ants. Let's sit here and watch the ants go <u>by</u>.

Cc

cake   Everybody had <u>cake</u> at the birthday party.

call   I heard someone <u>call</u> for help. So I made a phone <u>call</u> to the police.

came   Jim <u>came</u> to my house on Saturday.   Look at **come.**

can   **1** Tommy <u>can</u> stand on his head. **2** Will you open this <u>can</u> of beans for me?

candy   <u>Candy</u> is sweet because it has sugar in it.

car		cold

car

cat

catch   caught, catching Throw
the ball, and I will catch it. But
first button your coat, or you
will catch a cold.

caught   Jill caught the ball. She
also caught a cold playing in
the rain. Look at **catch.**

cave   Bears live in a cave in the
side of that mountain.

chair   chairs

cheek   Charles gave his aunt a
kiss on the cheek.

children   Children cannot go into
the deep end of the pool.

church   Marcie and I went to
church on Sunday.

circus   Sally liked the elephant in
the circus.

city   cities Sarah lives in the
country. I live in the city.

clap   clapped, clapping Count
to three. Then clap your hands.

clay   Joe made a rabbit out of
clay.

clean   Make sure your hands
are clean before you eat. Use
this soap to clean them.

clock

clown

cold   My hands and feet feel
cold. I think I am getting a
cold.

196

| color | doctor |

color What <u>color</u> is the sun? You should <u>color</u> the sun yellow.

come came, **coming** Will you <u>come</u> with me to the store?

cook Dad will <u>cook</u> dinner tonight. He is a good <u>cook</u>.

cookie You may have a <u>cookie</u> and some milk.

corner Turn right at the <u>corner</u>.

cost cost, **costing** These gloves <u>cost</u> three dollars.

could Pedro wishes he <u>could</u> run faster.

cow

crash **crashes** There was a loud <u>crash</u> when the dishes fell.

crawl Babies <u>crawl</u> before they can walk.

cross Look both ways before you <u>cross</u> the street.

cup

cut cut, **cutting** Jeff will <u>cut</u> the pie into six pieces.

D d

dad My mom and <u>dad</u> read a lot of books.

day Owls sleep during the <u>day</u>. One <u>day</u> last week I saw an owl at the zoo.

dear Nina began the letter with "<u>Dear</u> Olga."

deep We looked down into the well. It was very <u>deep</u>.

desk

did Karen <u>did</u> magic tricks at the party. What <u>did</u> Sam do? Look at **do.**

dig dug, **digging** Get a shovel and help me <u>dig</u> this hole.

dinner We eat <u>dinner</u> at 6:00.

dish **dishes** First help me wash these <u>dishes</u>. Then you may give the dog a <u>dish</u> of water.

do did, **doing, done** I can <u>do</u> this puzzle. <u>Do</u> you want to help me?

doctor I go to a <u>doctor</u> when I am sick.

does	end

does   Andy <u>does</u> his homework after supper. <u>Does</u> his mother help him?

dog

dollar   Gail gave Mark ten dimes for a <u>dollar</u>.

done   Have you <u>done</u> your spelling lesson? Look at **do.**

door   Knock first, then open the <u>door</u>.

down   We hiked up one side of the mountain and <u>down</u> the other.

draw   **drew, drawing** Steven likes to <u>draw</u> pictures of boats.

dream   What do you <u>dream</u> about? Once I had a <u>dream</u> about spaceships.

dress   **1 dresses** Pam has a new <u>dress</u> for the party. **2** My younger brother can <u>dress</u> himself.

drink   **drank, drinking** Please don't <u>drink</u> all the lemonade. You may have a <u>drink</u> of water.

drop   **1 dropped, dropping** The glass will break if you <u>drop</u> it. **2** I felt a <u>drop</u> of rain.

dry   **1 dried, drying** You wash the dishes and I will <u>dry</u> them. **2** Please get me a <u>dry</u> towel.

duck

dust   Everything in the old house was covered with <u>dust</u>.

E e

each   <u>Each</u> of us won a prize.

early   Mimi got up <u>early</u>. She wanted to get to school <u>early</u>.

earth   We planted the seeds in the <u>earth</u>.

easy   Everyone passed the test. It was an <u>easy</u> test.

eat   **ate, eating** I <u>eat</u> breakfast every morning.

egg

eight   The word for **8.**

empty   One glass was full. The other glass was <u>empty</u>.

end   We saw the <u>end</u> of the boat race. We watched from the <u>end</u> of the dock.

| ever | flower |

ever   Have you <u>ever</u> been to the circus?

F f

face   Kim has a smile on her <u>face</u>.

fall   **1 fell, falling** Be careful you don't <u>fall</u>. **2** School begins in the <u>fall</u>.

family   **families** Everyone in my <u>family</u> has red hair.

far   Tonio lives <u>far</u> away in another country.

farm

fast   The winner of the race ran very <u>fast</u>. She is a <u>fast</u> runner.

fat   If you feed your dog too much, he will get <u>fat</u>.

father   Monica's <u>father</u> is a teacher.

feel   **felt, feeling** Inez didn't <u>feel</u> well. Her mother <u>felt</u> her forehead to see if it was warm.

feet   **1** Nick got his <u>feet</u> wet in the puddle. **2** Lisa is almost four <u>feet</u> tall.

fell   Brad <u>fell</u> off his bike. Look at **fall.**

felt   Clark <u>felt</u> cold. The blanket <u>felt</u> warm and soft.   Look at **feel.**

fill   Let's <u>fill</u> this pail with sand.

find   **found, finding** Tim lost his book. He can't <u>find</u> it.

fine   Suki just got over a cold. She feels <u>fine</u> now.

finish   You may go out after you <u>finish</u> your homework.

fire   The forest <u>fire</u> burned down many trees.

fish

fit   This coat is too small. It does not <u>fit</u> me. Maybe it will <u>fit</u> my younger brother.

five   The word for **5.**

fix   Otis will <u>fix</u> the broken kite.

flat   **1** The top of a table is <u>flat</u>. **2** Fran fixed the <u>flat</u> tire.

flavor   I can taste the <u>flavor</u> of apples in my cereal.

flew   The bird <u>flew</u> away. I <u>flew</u> my kite.   Look at **fly.**

float   A piece of wood can <u>float</u> on water. A rock cannot <u>float</u>.

flower   Rosa picked a red <u>flower</u> in the garden.

fly 1 flew, flying Jet planes <u>fly</u> very high. I can <u>fly</u> my kite high. **2 flies** A big <u>fly</u> buzzed outside the window.

follow You go first, and I will <u>follow</u> you.

foot feet 1 The big toe on my left <u>foot</u> hurts. **2** There are 12 inches in a <u>foot</u>.

football

for I have a present <u>for</u> you.

forgot Len knew her first name, but he <u>forgot</u> her last name.

found Jean <u>found</u> a dollar bill on the sidewalk. Look at **find.**

fox foxes

free 1 The magic show is <u>free</u>. We don't have to pay to go. **2** Mom isn't busy now. She has some <u>free</u> time.

friend Don is my best <u>friend</u>.

frighten Don't move or you will <u>frighten</u> the deer away.

frog

from Is it far <u>from</u> your house to the park? Can you get some money <u>from</u> your brother?

front There was a line in <u>front</u> of the store. Marsha was at the <u>front</u> of the line.

full There is no more room in this box. It is <u>full</u>.

fun We had <u>fun</u> at the circus.

funny We all laughed at the <u>funny</u> joke.

G g

game Let's play a <u>game</u> of tag.

gave Sandy <u>gave</u> me a paint set for my birthday. Look at **give.**

get got, getting 1 What did you <u>get</u> for your birthday? **2** When did you <u>get</u> up this morning?

girl That <u>girl</u> is in my class. Her name is Kathy.

give gave, giving What did you <u>give</u> Sara for her birthday?

glad I am <u>glad</u> to see you.

glass glasses 1 A rock broke the <u>glass</u> in the window. **2** Jed had a <u>glass</u> of milk. **3** My dad wears <u>glasses</u> when he reads.

| go | have |

go **went, going, gone** Hal wants to go for a ride. I am going to go with him.

goat

gold This ring is made of gold.

gone The party is over. Everyone has gone home. All the food is gone. Look at **go.**

good These carrots taste good. They are good for you, too.

goodness He showed his goodness by helping people.

got **1** Nora got a train set for her birthday. **2** Juan got home before dark. Look at **get.**

grand The prince lived in a grand old palace.

grass

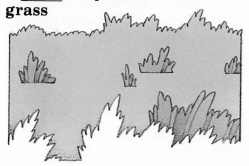

great The party was in a great big house. We had a great time.

grew Emma grew flowers in her garden. But weeds grew there, too. Look at **grow.**

ground The rain made the ground wet and muddy.

grow **grew, growing** Eric and Jerry grow tomatoes. Some of the plants grow very tall.

H h

had Holly had a pencil, but she lost it. Look at **have.**

hall Our classroom is at the end of the hall.

hand

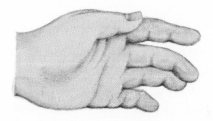

hang **hung, hanging** Bats hang upside down when they sleep. You hung the picture upside down.

happy Our class won the prize. Our teacher was very happy.

hard This rock is hard. It is hard to break it with a hammer.

hardly It hardly ever rains in the desert.

has Todd has a blue bike, and I have a red one. Look at **have.**

have **had, having** Chad and Mindy have new skates.

he

he   Warren fell down, but <u>he</u> didn't get hurt.

hear   **heard, hearing** I <u>hear</u> the telephone ringing.

heard   We <u>heard</u> a loud noise outside.   Look at **hear.**

hello   Do you say "<u>hello</u>" when you answer the phone?

help   Will you <u>help</u> me rake the leaves? I can use some <u>help</u>.

hen

her   Glenda carries <u>her</u> books in a bag. I saw <u>her</u> this morning.

here   You stay <u>here</u>, and I will go over there.

hide   **hid, hiding** Let's <u>hide</u> behind this tree. Then we can see where they <u>hide</u> the gold.

high   Planes fly very <u>high</u> in the sky.

hill

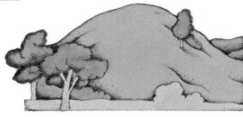

him   Carla waved to Fred when she saw <u>him</u>.

in

his   Tom let me use <u>his</u> bat.

hit   **hit, hitting** John <u>hit</u> the ball into right field. It was the first <u>hit</u> of the game.

hold   **held, holding** <u>Hold</u> this big pail with two hands. It <u>holds</u> a lot of water.

home   Nat stayed <u>home</u> yesterday.

hope   **hoped, hoping** I <u>hope</u> you find your cat. You must not give up <u>hope</u>.

house

how   Show me <u>how</u> you did that trick. <u>How</u> long did it take to learn it?

hungry   I didn't feed the cats today. They must be <u>hungry</u>.

hurt   **hurt, hurting** Jack fell off the swing and <u>hurt</u> himself.

I i

I   My name is Pete. <u>I</u> am eight years old.

if   We can go <u>if</u> it stops raining. I don't know <u>if</u> Matt is coming.

in   There is too much sugar <u>in</u> the lemonade.

is		learn

is Fern <u>is</u> my friend. She <u>is</u> staying with me for two weeks.

it Ned has a new kite. <u>It</u> is red and black.

J j

jar

jet Martha flew from Portland to Chicago on a <u>jet</u>.

job Edith got a <u>job</u> in a store.

joke Jason told us a funny <u>joke</u>.

jump My dog can <u>jump</u> over this fence.

just I got to school <u>just</u> before the bell rang.

K k

keep kept, keeping Missy found a puppy. She wants to <u>keep</u> it. But it <u>keeps</u> running away.

key

kick If the gate sticks, <u>kick</u> it with your foot.

kind **1** Most people are <u>kind</u> to small animals. **2** What <u>kind</u> of animals do you like?

kitchen Our family eats breakfast in the <u>kitchen</u>.

kite

kitten The mother cat played with her <u>kitten</u>.

know knew, knowing I <u>know</u> her name, but I don't <u>know</u> where she lives.

L l

lake We rowed the boat across the <u>lake</u>.

large An elephant is a very <u>large</u> animal.

last December is the <u>last</u> month of the year. I was seven years old <u>last</u> December.

late Dirk got home <u>late</u> last night. He was <u>late</u> for school this morning.

laugh People <u>laugh</u> when they hear something funny.

learn What did you <u>learn</u> in school today?

| leave | made |

leave **left, leaving** Please be careful as you <u>leave</u> the plane. Make sure you don't <u>leave</u> anything behind.

left **1** Doug writes with his <u>left</u> hand. **2** I <u>left</u> before the movie was over. I <u>left</u> my gloves on the seat. Look at **leave.**

leg How long can you stand on one <u>leg</u>?

let **let, letting** Mom <u>let</u> me go on a butterfly hunt. <u>Let</u> go of my net! Oh, you <u>let</u> the butterfly get away!

letter **1** My baby sister knows every <u>letter</u> in the alphabet. **2** Now she wants to write a <u>letter</u> to the President!

life **lives** That big turtle at the zoo is 90 years old. It has had a very long <u>life</u>.

lift Bend your knees when you <u>lift</u> something heavy.

like **1** I <u>like</u> bread. I even <u>like</u> to bake it. **2** Becky looks just <u>like</u> her mother.

lion

listen You should <u>listen</u> when someone speaks to you.

little Polly found a <u>little</u> gray kitten. She gave it a <u>little</u> milk in a saucer.

live **lived, living** Liz and her mother <u>live</u> in a small town in Oregon.

live We saw a <u>live</u> TV show in California.

lock This key opens the <u>lock</u> on the gate. Be sure you <u>lock</u> it when you leave.

long Stan made a kite with a <u>long</u> tail. It took him a <u>long</u> time to make it.

look <u>Look</u> at all those people down there. They <u>look</u> like ants.

lost Frank <u>lost</u> the baseball game. Then he <u>lost</u> his new watch. So he went for a walk, but he got <u>lost</u>.

lot Amy had a <u>lot</u> of flower seeds. So she planted some of them in the empty <u>lot</u>.

low Lucy bumped her head on a <u>low</u> tree branch.

luck Mrs. Cramer wished me <u>luck</u> before the contest.

lucky Rob fell off his bike. He was <u>lucky</u> he didn't get hurt.

lunch Alice and I eat <u>lunch</u> together at school.

Mm

mad Fritz gets <u>mad</u> when his brother teases him.

made Sally <u>made</u> a bird house. Look at **make.**

mail

mail I didn't get your letter in the mail. Did you forget to mail it?

make made, making Carlos can make a hat out of paper.

man men The tall man in the middle is my father.

many There are many stars in the sky.

may 1 You may stay up late and watch TV. **2** George was born on May 18.

maybe Vicky is not here yet. Maybe she got lost.

me Peter told me a story.

mean 1 meant, meaning What does that big word mean? **2** People who hurt animals are mean.

men More than one man. The men wore suits and ties.

middle Your nose is in the middle of your face.

milk Brenda had a glass of milk with her sandwich.

mirror

miss 1 My best friend moved away. I miss her. I can't even play basketball. I miss the basket every time. **2** My new teacher is Miss Ortiz.

nail

mix If you mix yellow and blue, you get green.

month The first month of the year is January.

more Lester has 10 pennies. Vera has 12. Vera has more pennies than Lester.

morning The sun comes up in the morning.

moss That green stuff growing on the rocks is moss.

most The player with the most points wins the game.

mother Ed's mother is a doctor.

mouse mice

much There is too much salt in the soup. How much did you put in?

must Everyone must try hard to win.

my This is my desk. Your desk is over there.

myself I painted a picture of myself.

N n

nail

| near | over |

near Debbie lives next door. Keith lives <u>near</u> me, too.

neat The papers were stacked in a <u>neat</u> pile.

neck A giraffe has a very long <u>neck</u>.

need I <u>need</u> some paper and a pencil to write a letter.

nest

new We sold our old car and bought a <u>new</u> one.

next Dinah sits <u>next</u> to me in school. <u>Next</u> year we will not be in the same class.

nice What a <u>nice</u> day for a hike in the woods!

night The moon and stars come out at <u>night</u>.

no I have <u>no</u> money. Will you give me some? <u>No</u>, I won't.

nose I hold my <u>nose</u> when I jump into the pool.

note **1** Jane wrote a <u>note</u> to Paula. **2** Paco played a wrong <u>note</u> on the piano.

now Do your homework <u>now</u>. You can play later.

oak

oatmeal Hot <u>oatmeal</u> tastes good on a cold morning.

of The door <u>of</u> the house was open. It was made <u>of</u> wood.

off Take <u>off</u> your shoes. Turn <u>off</u> the light and go to sleep.

on Turn <u>on</u> the light. Put <u>on</u> your glasses and read a book.

or Answer each question with yes <u>or</u> no.

order **1** Put the words in ABC <u>order</u>. **2** The captain gave the <u>order</u> to march.

other I found one shoe, but I can't find the <u>other</u> one.

our My sister and I made a cake for <u>our</u> mother's birthday.

outside We went <u>outside</u> after the rain stopped.

over **1** A large jet flew <u>over</u> the house. I put my hands <u>over</u> my ears. **2** We left before the game was <u>over</u>.

owl

owl

own   I wish I could <u>own</u> a bike shop. Then I would fix my <u>own</u> bicycle.

P p

page   Read the story that begins on <u>page</u> 21.

paint   Will you help me <u>paint</u> the fence? You can use the red <u>paint</u>.

pan

pants   Jeremy got a new pair of <u>pants</u>.

park   **1** Our class had a picnic in the <u>park</u>. **2** You can <u>park</u> the car by the gate.

part   Your knee is a <u>part</u> of your leg.

plain

pass   **1** You can <u>pass</u> the test if you study. **2** We watched the parade <u>pass</u> by.

past   We have lived in this house for the <u>past</u> four years.

pat   patted, patting You may <u>pat</u> the dog on the head. But give it a gentle <u>pat</u>.

path   We followed the <u>path</u> through the woods.

paw   The cat licked its front <u>paw</u>.

pay   paid, paying How much did you <u>pay</u> for that ring?

penny   pennies

person   We must find the <u>person</u> who did this.

pet   petted, petting I like to <u>pet</u> my hamster Curly. He is a fine <u>pet</u>.

pick   <u>Pick</u> any card you want. Then <u>pick</u> it up. But don't let me see it.

pig

place   placed, placing <u>Place</u> the fork next to the plate. That is the <u>place</u> for it.

plain   Chet wrapped the box in <u>plain</u> paper.

| plant | return |

plant José gave me a bean plant. But I don't know where to plant it.

play 1 Who wants to play tag with me? 2 Susie has a big part in the school play.

playground

please Say please when you ask for something.

pond A pond is a small lake.

pop popped, popping Let's pop some popcorn. I love to hear it pop.

pretty What a pretty new dress you have!

prize Carmen won first prize in the spelling contest.

pull You get in the wagon and I'll pull it.

push The car is stuck. We will have to push it. Give it a big push.

put 'put, putting Ronald put a dime in his bank.

R r

rabbit

raccoon

race raced, racing Do you want to race me? We can have a race around the block.

rain 1 It is going to rain this evening. 2 We need the rain.

ran A little mouse ran across the room. Look at **run.**

real Monsters are make-believe. But big brown bears are real.

rest 1 If you are tired, you should rest. 2 You can do the rest of the work tomorrow.

return In the spring, geese return to their homes in the north.

| ride | set |

Ss

ride   rode, riding Rick taught me how to <u>ride</u> a horse. We go for a <u>ride</u> every Sunday.

right   1 Judy writes with her <u>right</u> hand. **2** I got the answer <u>right</u> away. **3** I knew it was <u>right</u>.

ring   rang, ringing 1 I heard the school bell <u>ring</u>. **2** Marnie wears a silver <u>ring</u>.

road   We drove down a bumpy <u>road</u>.

roast   We had <u>roast</u> beef for dinner.

robin

room   You can put your sleeping bag in my <u>room</u>. But I don't have <u>room</u> for your bike.

rope   We need some <u>rope</u> to tie up this box. May we use your jump <u>rope</u>?

round   Baseballs, oranges, and the moon are <u>round</u>.

row   1 Erica planted a <u>row</u> of beans in the garden. **2** I can't <u>row</u> the boat without oars.

rub   rubbed, rubbing If your hands are cold, <u>rub</u> them together.

run   ran, running A deer can <u>run</u> very fast. How fast can you <u>run</u>?

safe   She felt <u>safe</u> on the plane. She had a <u>safe</u> trip.

said   Kelly <u>said</u> she would meet us at noon.   Look at **say.**

same   My book is the <u>same</u> as Vinnie's book.

sat   Josh <u>sat</u> on a bench and fed the birds.   Look at **sit.**

save   saved, saving 1 I <u>save</u> old bottle tops. **2** My aunt <u>saved</u> the boy from drowning.

saw   Henry <u>saw</u> that movie three times.   Look at **see.**

saw

say   said, saying What did you <u>say</u>? I didn't hear what you <u>said</u>.

school   I learn a lot of things in <u>school</u>.

see   saw, seeing You can <u>see</u> the parade better if you stand here. I <u>see</u> what you mean.

seed   Ronnie found a <u>seed</u> in her orange juice.

sent   My father <u>sent</u> a letter to the newspaper.

set   set, setting 1 The sun will <u>set</u> at 6:30 today. **2** Amos has a new <u>set</u> of paints.

shake | sky

shake shook, shaking We felt the earthquake <u>shake</u> the house. Everything in the room <u>shook</u>.

she Diana studies a lot. <u>She</u> gets good grades.

sheep

shell

shine 1 shone, shining The stars seem to <u>shine</u> brighter in the country. **2 shined, shining** Marty <u>shined</u> his shoes.

shoe

shook Heather <u>shook</u> the bottle before she opened it. Look at **shake.**

shop shopped, shopping Carrie likes to <u>shop</u> in the morning. The <u>shops</u> are not busy then.

short Dennis got his hair cut <u>short</u>.

should You <u>should</u> write Grandma a letter.

shout I can hear you. You don't need to <u>shout</u>.

show I want to <u>show</u> you my picture. It is going to be in the art <u>show</u>.

shut shut, shutting Please <u>shut</u> the door when you leave. All the windows in the house are already <u>shut</u>.

shy Kirby is <u>shy</u> in front of strangers.

sick Wanda is <u>sick</u> in bed with a cold. She is <u>sick</u> of staying in bed.

side Bobby bumped into the <u>side</u> of the door. He hurt his left side.

sight Julie hid behind a rock. She was out of <u>sight</u>.

sing sang, singing We started to <u>sing</u> songs at the party. My friends said I <u>sang</u> well.

sister My older <u>sister</u> helps me with my homework.

sit sat, sitting Let's <u>sit</u> under that tree and talk.

skate skated, skating Rico taught me how to <u>skate</u>. He even let me use his <u>skates</u>.

sky White fluffy clouds floated in the <u>sky</u>.

sleep	step

sleep   slept, sleeping Jamie likes to <u>sleep</u> in a tent. Sometimes he doesn't get much <u>sleep</u>.

slide   slid, sliding Big rocks sometimes <u>slide</u> down the hill.

slow   Turtles are very <u>slow</u> animals.

small   Elephants are big. Ants are <u>small</u>.

smile   smiled, smiling Look at the camera and <u>smile</u>. That's a nice <u>smile</u>.

snake

so   Ken hit the ball <u>so</u> hard, he broke his bat. <u>So</u> he had to use my bat.

soap   Arthur washed his socks in <u>soap</u> and warm water.

soft   My cat's fur is very <u>soft</u>.

some   Most birds fly, but <u>some</u> birds cannot fly.

son   Dad is Grandpa's <u>son</u>.

song   Let's sing a <u>song</u> we all know.

soon   It is almost nighttime. <u>Soon</u> it will be dark.

sound   I didn't make a <u>sound</u>. The deer came right up to me. That <u>sounds</u> exciting.

spell   Tracy knows how to <u>spell</u> Mississippi.

spend   spent, spending How much money did you <u>spend</u> today?

spoke   **1** Mark <u>spoke</u> to Paul on the phone. **2** Raul bent a <u>spoke</u> in the front wheel of his bike.

spoon

spot   **1** Sharon got a <u>spot</u> of ink on her dress. **2** This is a great <u>spot</u> for a picnic.

stand   stood, standing When you hear your name, <u>stand</u> up.

stare   stared, staring My dog likes to <u>stare</u> at birds.

start   I hope they don't <u>start</u> the race without me. I want to be there right at the <u>start</u>.

stay   Claire had to <u>stay</u> after school.

steep   The hill was too <u>steep</u> for us to climb.

step   stepped, stepping Take a giant <u>step</u>. Don't <u>step</u> in the puddle. Then sit on the <u>steps</u> and wait for me.

stick

stick **1 stuck, sticking** Stamps will stick together if they get wet. **2** Ella wrote her name in the sand with a stick.

still **1** The rabbit stood very still. **2** It was still there when we left.

stone David threw a stone in the water.

stood We stood in line for an hour. Look at **stand.**

stop **stopped, stopping** Mom stopped the car. She would not start again until we stopped fighting.

store Dick went to the store to buy milk.

story **stories** Jessica wrote a story about a flying saucer.

stove

straight Howie drew a straight line. He drew it straight across the paper.

straw I like to drink milk with a straw.

street The street was crowded with cars and buses.

string Beth tied a very long piece of string to her kite.

strong Jake is strong. He can lift his bike with one hand.

teach

stuff **1** Don't stuff your mittens in your pockets. **2** Put all your stuff in this bag.

sugar Sugar makes things taste sweet.

summer Summer is the hottest time of the year.

sunny People go to the beach when it is warm and sunny.

sweater

sweet The apples had a sweet taste.

swim **swam, swimming** Do you know how to swim? Let's go for a swim now.

T t

tail A pig has a curly tail. Birds, kites, and airplanes have tails, too.

talk Did your parents talk to you about your report card? Yes, we had a long talk.

tall There are many tall buildings in Chicago.

taught My grandmother taught school for 40 years. Look at **teach.**

teach **taught, teaching** Will you teach me how to draw?

teeth

teeth I brush my <u>teeth</u> after every meal.

tell told, telling You should never <u>tell</u> a lie.

ten The word for **10.**

test Our teacher gave us a spelling <u>test</u> today.

than Libby is taller <u>than</u> Cindy.

thank <u>Thank</u> you for helping me.

that <u>That</u> boy is strange. He says <u>that</u> he is from outer space.

the <u>The</u> top of <u>the</u> mountain was covered with snow.

their The monkeys hung by <u>their</u> tails in the cage.

them I have three cats. I feed <u>them</u> twice a day.

then First wash your hands. <u>Then</u> you may eat.

there <u>There</u> is no room here. You will have to sit over <u>there</u> near the door.

these <u>These</u> books are mine. Your books are over there on the desk.

they Max and Bill are tired. <u>They</u> worked very hard today in the garden.

thing What is that <u>thing</u> on the back of your bike?

think thought, thinking <u>Think</u> carefully before you answer. I <u>think</u> you know the answer to the question.

this <u>This</u> button turns it on. That one turns it off.

together

those <u>Those</u> glasses on the table belong to my father. These are mine.

thought I <u>thought</u> you were coming with us.   Look at **think.**

three The word for **3.**

throw threw, throwing <u>Throw</u> the ball over here. That was a good <u>throw</u>.

thumb Your <u>thumb</u> is a part of your hand.

tie 1 tied, tying Sailors know how to <u>tie</u> many kinds of knots. **2** Jim wore a suit and <u>tie</u> to the party. **3** The game ended in a <u>tie</u>.

tiger

time What <u>time</u> is it? Do we have <u>time</u> for one more game?

tire The car has a flat <u>tire</u>.

to Carla went <u>to</u> the store. She wanted <u>to</u> buy a present.

toad

toast Peg burned the <u>toast</u> and spilled the milk.

today Nelson was sick yesterday, but he is fine <u>today</u>.

together Bruce, Adam, and Mike went to the park <u>together</u>.

told	try

told   Penny <u>told</u> me the answer.   Look at **tell.**

too   It is <u>too</u> cold to ride our bikes. It is going to rain, <u>too</u>.

took   We <u>took</u> all the books off the shelves. It <u>took</u> us a long time to do it.

top   **1** The climbers reached the <u>top</u> of the mountain. **2** A <u>top</u> is a toy that you can spin.

torn   A page in my book is <u>torn</u>. I will fix it with some tape.

tower

town   Chris lives in a small <u>town</u> in Utah.

toy   Everyone brought a <u>toy</u> for the grab bag.

track   Flowers and weeds grew along the railroad <u>track</u>.

trail   The hikers followed the <u>trail</u> through the woods.

train

trap   trapped, trapping We tried to <u>trap</u> the mouse. We put cheese in the <u>trap</u>.

treat   **1** You should <u>treat</u> people with kindness. **2** Let me <u>treat</u> you to an ice cream cone. That's a nice <u>treat</u>!

tree

trick   Barbara taught me a new magic <u>trick</u>.

truck

true   This story is not make-believe. It is a <u>true</u> story.

trunk   **1** The elephant picked up the peanut with its <u>trunk</u>. **2** I leaned against the <u>trunk</u> of the tree. **3** We put the suitcases in the <u>trunk</u> of the car.

trust   I won't tell your secret. You can <u>trust</u> me.

try   tried, trying I will <u>try</u> to call you tomorrow.

turn

turn 1 Turn around and close your eyes. **2** It is my turn to hide and your turn to find me.

twice Hilda ran around the block not one time, but twice.

Uu

until We waited until the rain stopped.

up Dad climbed up the ladder. My kite was up on the roof.

us We laughed at the monkeys, and they laughed at us.

use used, using Greg knows how to use chopsticks.

Vv

very The sun is very hot.

visit Should we visit Gary at his store? I think he will enjoy our visit.

Ww

wait We had to wait half an hour for a bus.

walk My friends and I walk to school every day. It is a nice walk through the park.

wall Thad hung his picture on the wall.

want I know what I want for my birthday. But I don't want to tell you.

was Dale was late for school. He was watching a bird build a nest.

wash Bonnie and I will wash the dishes.

watch We can watch the parade from the window.

watch

water Fill this pail with water. Then you can water the plants.

wave 1 waved, waving Wave to the people in the boat. **2** Don't let that big wave knock you over.

way This is the shortest way to the library.

we Denise and I went to the zoo. We had a great time.

weather I hope we have good weather for the picnic.

well Hank can sing very well. But he doesn't sing when he is not feeling well.

went Cissy went home early. Look at **go**.

were We were the first ones at the party. Marla and Ross were making the lemonade.

wet I got wet in the rain.

what What is that? I don't know what it is.

when When does the party begin? It begins when you get here.

| where | your |

where   Where did she go? She
didn't tell me where she went.

who   Who is that? I don't know
who that is.

why   Why did he do that? I don't
know why he did that.

wide   The river is very wide. Do
you know how wide it is?

window

winter   Winter is the coldest
time of the year.

wise   A wise person knows
many things.

wish   If you had one wish, what
would you wish for?

with   I want a bike with two
seats. Then you could ride with
me.

woke   I woke up in the middle
of the night. I heard a noise, so
I woke my father.

woman   **women** That woman
over there is my Aunt Mary.

won   Janice got the most points.
She won the game.

wonder   I wonder what I will be
when I grow up.

wood   Some houses are made of
wood.

wool   Wool comes from sheep. I
have a warm wool coat.

word   Hector looked up the new
word in his dictionary.

work   My uncles work in a
garage. It is hard work. But
they like to make broken cars
work.

world   Many kinds of people
live in the world.

would   What would you like to
do now?

write   **wrote, writing** Curt said
he would write me a letter
every week. I wrote him a letter
last week.

wrong   I get mad when I give a
wrong answer. Is it wrong for
me to get mad?

yard   **1** We have trees in our
yard. **2** There are three feet in
a yard.

year   There are 365 days in a
year.

yes   Answer the question with
yes or no. Do you understand?
Yes.

yet   Becky is here, but Ricardo
is not here yet.

you   You are my best friend.

young   A young bear is called a
cub.

your   You may keep that pencil.
It is your pencil now.

WORD BOOK
Same and Opposite Words

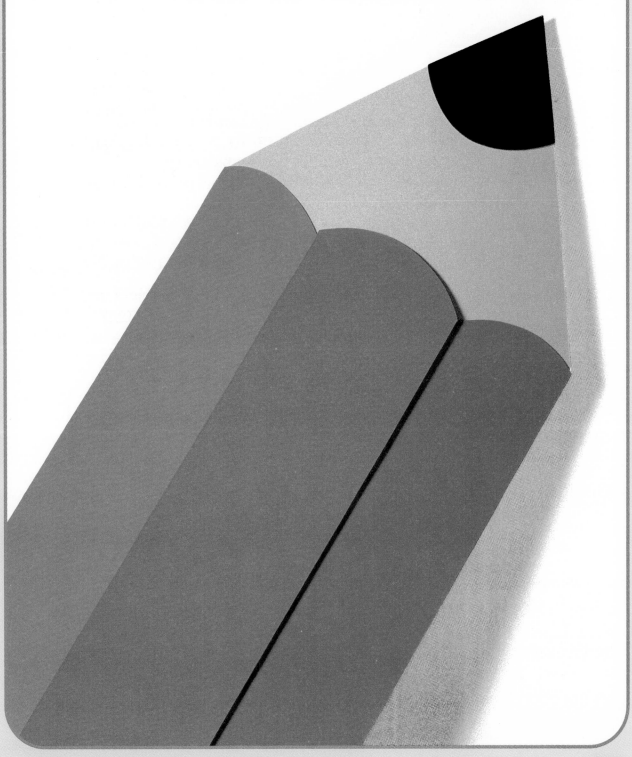

Your Word Book

The Word Book is a list of words. The words are in ABC order. Each of these words is called an **entry word.** The Word Book lists words that mean the same as the entry words. Sometimes the Word Book lists opposites.

Look at this example from the Word Book.

The **entry word** is red. It is used in a sentence.

> fast — The rabbit was too fast for the dog to catch.

Words that mean almost the same as the entry word are in a list. Each word is used in a sentence.

> quick — The quick fox ran into the forest.
> speedy — The speedy car won the race.
> swift — The swift bird flew away from the cat.

An **opposite** is also listed.

> **OPPOSITE:** slow

How to Use Your Word Book

You write some sentences about an airplane. You read your sentences. You see you used the word <u>fast</u> too much. Use the Word Book to find words that mean almost the same as <u>fast</u>. Follow these steps.

1. Find the word fast. Remember that words in the Word Book are in ABC order. To find fast, look under the letter **F.**

2. Read the entry carefully. Choose the words from the list that will make your writing clearer and stronger.

Remember: Not every word in the list will have the meaning you want. Look at the example on page 218. Which words from the list for fast would fit best in sentences about an airplane?

afraid		brave

A

afraid	Jim is afraid to climb the tree.
frightened	The frightened cat ran from the loud noise.
scared	Chris was not scared to walk into the dark cave.

OPPOSITES: bold, brave, daring

angry	When I am angry, I go for a walk.
cross	Tim is cross because he lost his baseball.
furious	The new lamp is broken. My father is furious.

OPPOSITES: calm, glad, happy, pleased

awful	Your muddy clothes look awful.
bad	There was a bad storm last night.
terrible	The smoke from the fire smelled terrible.

See also **bad.**
OPPOSITES: good, pleasant

B

bad	The sour milk tasted bad.
awful	The old potato salad smelled awful.

rotten	Don't eat that rotten apple.
spoiled	The soup left on the stove last night has spoiled.

See also **awful.**
OPPOSITES: delicious, good, pleasant, tasty

big	The big man lifted the box for us.
giant	The giant elephant ate the tiny peanut.
grand	They went to a party in a grand hotel.
great	The great tree fell with a crash.
large	Let's cut that large apple and share it.
tall	Most basketball players are very tall.

OPPOSITES: little, short, small, tiny

boat	The boat floated down the river.
rowboat	They rowed their rowboat to the middle of the lake.
sailboat	She put up the sail on her sailboat.
ship	The ship was much bigger than the sailboat.

brave	The brave girl fed the whale a fish.

bright

bold	The <u>bold</u> squirrel dashed out for more nuts.
daring	<u>Daring</u> men flew the first planes.
fearless	The lion trainer was <u>fearless</u>.

OPPOSITES: fearful, frightened, scared

bright	The sun is very bright today.
brilliant	The leaves on the trees had <u>brilliant</u> colors.
shining	The <u>shining</u> headlights showed the road was clear.

OPPOSITES: dark, dim, dull

C

call	We call her name, but she doesn't answer.
cry	The boy in the story will <u>cry</u> for help.
howl	The wolves <u>howl</u> their sad cries to the moon.
scream	Babies often <u>scream</u> when they are hungry.
shout	We <u>shout</u> for our team when they win.
yell	Sue had to <u>yell</u> over the noise of the train.

OPPOSITE: whisper

catch	<u>Catch</u> the ball when I throw it to you.

deep

grab	<u>Grab</u> your glass of milk before it spills.
grasp	I tried to <u>grasp</u> the pen before it fell.

OPPOSITES: drop, throw

cold	Put on a coat so you will not be cold.
cool	The open window let in a <u>cool</u> breeze.
icy	I blew on my <u>icy</u> hands to warm them.

OPPOSITES: hot, mild, warm

cook	Sarah will cook the turkey in the oven.
bake	Let's <u>bake</u> bread today.
boil	<u>Boil</u> the eggs for three minutes.
fry	<u>Fry</u> the fish in this pan.
roast	Please <u>roast</u> the chicken in the oven.

cut	Please cut your paper in two.
carve	Mother can <u>carve</u> the meat at the dinner table.
chop	Jeff must <u>chop</u> the wood for the fire.
trim	Butchers <u>trim</u> fat from meat.

D

deep	We could not see the bottom of the deep pond.

eat

| bottomless | Mike dove into a lake that looked <u>bottomless</u>. |
| low | There were mountains around the <u>low</u> valley. |

OPPOSITE: high

E

eat	We eat dinner at six o'clock.
feast	Our family likes to <u>feast</u> with friends on Thanksgiving.
feed	Horses <u>feed</u> on hay and oats.
gobble	The dogs <u>gobble</u> their breakfast.
nibble	I saw some deer <u>nibble</u> on my plants.
taste	May I <u>taste</u> what you are cooking?

F

fall	Leaves fall when the days get cool.
drop	Please don't <u>drop</u> the eggs.
sink	That toy boat will <u>sink</u> in the tub.
trip	Jason's shoes are untied. He may <u>trip</u>.
tumble	We watched the clown <u>tumble</u> over and over.

OPPOSITES: climb, rise

	fill

fast	The rabbit was too fast for the dog to catch.
quick	The <u>quick</u> fox ran into the forest.
speedy	The <u>speedy</u> car won the race.
swift	The <u>swift</u> bird flew away from the cat.

OPPOSITE: slow

fat	Winnie-the-Pooh was fat because he ate too much honey.
overweight	The doctor said my brother was not <u>overweight</u> for his age.
stout	The <u>stout</u> clown couldn't fit in the car.

OPPOSITES: slender, thin

feel	These blankets feel soft.
handle	<u>Handle</u> the baby gently when you hold her.
touch	Don't <u>touch</u> the hot pot.

fill	Please fill the glass with milk.
load	Father will <u>load</u> the car for our picnic.
pack	I can <u>pack</u> my own things for camp.
stuff	We <u>stuff</u> all our toys in the closet.

OPPOSITES: empty, unload

<table>
<tr><td colspan="2">find</td></tr>
</table>

find	Please help me find my glasses.
catch	I try to <u>catch</u> words that I spelled wrong.
discover	Did you <u>discover</u> where your bicycle is?
uncover	We might <u>uncover</u> some old coins in the garden.

OPPOSITES: bury, hide, miss

fine	I was sick yesterday, but today I feel fine.
healthy	I always feel <u>healthy</u> when I walk.
well	You sound as if you have a cold. Do you feel <u>well</u>?

**OPPOSITES: awful, ill
sick**

fix	Erin can fix the broken clock.
patch	Julie will <u>patch</u> the hole in the wall.
repair	My grandparents <u>repair</u> broken windows.

**OPPOSITES: break, crack,
destroy**

flat	My mother makes thin, flat pancakes.
even	They use sandpaper to make the wood <u>even</u>.
smooth	We rode our bicycles easily down the <u>smooth</u> path.

**OPPOSITES: bumpy, rough,
uneven**

fly	Some birds fly south in the winter.
drift	We watched the snow <u>drift</u> to the ground.
float	Falling leaves <u>float</u> to the ground.
glide	The ducks <u>glide</u> down and land in the pond.
soar	The fast plane will <u>soar</u> into the sky.
frighten	Loud noises frighten babies.
scare	Did I <u>scare</u> you when I dropped the plate?
startle	If the dog barks, it will <u>startle</u> the baby.
full	I was full after I ate dinner.
crowded	People were standing on the <u>crowded</u> bus.
filled	The glass is <u>filled</u> with milk.
loaded	The horses slowly pulled the <u>loaded</u> hay wagon.
packed	The <u>packed</u> suitcase would not close.

OPPOSITE: empty

G

good	I eat chicken often because it tastes so good.

ground	

delicious | Apples and pears are delicious fruits.
fine | We enjoyed a fine dinner at my aunt's home.
great | Joe always brings a great lunch to school.

OPPOSITES: awful, bad, dreadful, terrible

ground | We dug a deep hole in the ground for a rose bush.
dirt | We covered the roots of the bush with dirt.
earth | You should water a plant when the earth around it is dry.

H

happy | I was happy to see my mother come home from her trip.
cheerful | Sunshine and flowers make me feel cheerful.
glad | My dog wags his tail to show he is glad to see me.
merry | The merry children raced into the yard to play.
pleased | My father was pleased that I had cleaned my room.

OPPOSITES: sad, unhappy

hard | Some parts of the test were hard.

	hold

difficult | It's difficult to give a dog a bath.
tough | Learning to ice skate can be tough.

OPPOSITES: easy, simple

hide | Where can we hide these presents?
bury | Squirrels bury nuts in the ground.
cover | Please cover the butter and put it away.

OPPOSITES: discover, find, show, uncover

hit | Can you hit a ball with a bat?
beat | The baby beat the pot with a spoon.
kick | Kick the soccer ball with the side of your foot.
knock | Please knock on the door before you come in.
pat | You can pat your face dry with this towel.
slap | Beavers slap the water with their tails.
strike | Don't strike your thumb with the hammer.
tap | Gary can tap a tune on the glass bottles.

hold | Can you hold this big box in your arms?

house

grasp — Grasp the bars so you don't fall.

grip — Did you grip the bat with both hands?

OPPOSITE: drop

house — My grandfather built our house many years ago.

cabin — Abraham Lincoln lived in a log cabin when he was a boy.

cottage — The cottage had only one bedroom.

hurt — Does the bee sting still hurt?

bruise — George may bruise his knee if he falls.

harm — Too much sun can harm your skin.

J

jump — Cleo can jump higher than anyone in the class.

hop — We watched a rabbit hop into the garden.

leap — My cat will leap over the chair.

spring — The diver was ready to spring from the diving board.

laugh

K

kind — A kind nurse took care of the sick child.

friendly — A friendly man helped my father fix my bike.

gentle — Be gentle when you hold small animals.

nice — Kathy helped me study. She is a nice sister.

tender — I gave the baby a tender pat.

warm — Our teacher gives us a warm smile every morning.

OPPOSITES: cold, cruel, mean, rough, unkind

L

lake — We went swimming in the clear lake.

pond — Mrs. Martin has two goldfish in her small pond.

pool — The rain made a pool of water in our yard.

puddle — A robin was taking a bath in a puddle.

laugh — The clowns made everyone laugh.

chuckle — My friends chuckle at my jokes.

giggle — Babies giggle when they are happy.

little

little — The little horse stayed by its mother.

short — The short woman could not reach the top shelf.

small — That small bug is a ladybug.

tiny — Large trees grow from tiny seeds.

OPPOSITES: big, giant, large, tall

M

make — Father and I make dinner together.

build — The robins build a nest with sticks and grass.

form — We must form a circle to play the game.

shape — Shape the clay into a dog.

OPPOSITES: break, destroy, ruin

mean — Dien is a kind boy. He is never mean to his pets.

bad — Don't do anything bad at school today.

cruel — The cruel giant tied up Jack.

unkind — It is unkind to hurt any pet.

OPPOSITES: good, kind, nice, tender

	pet

N

nice — The children played outdoors on nice days.

beautiful — It was a beautiful day for a picnic.

fair — The day was fair and warm.

fine — I enjoy walking on fine fall weekends.

lovely — It was a lovely day for a parade.

sunny — My family goes to the park when it is sunny.

OPPOSITES: awful, cloudy, rainy, terrible

O

order — Mother gave an order to clean our rooms.

command — The dog rolled over at the boy's command.

direction — Our teacher gave us a direction. He told us to write our names.

P

pet — You can pet a horse on its nose.

pat — Terese likes to pat her dog on the head.

stroke — I like to stroke a rabbit's soft fur.

plain

plain	I wrote my letter on plain white paper.
ordinary	Is that an ordinary watch?
simple	The girl wore a simple white dress to the party.

pretty	The pretty doll wears a pink dress.
beautiful	A beautiful swan is in the pond.
lovely	Lovely flowers grew in the garden.

pull	The boy can pull a wagon behind him.
drag	The chair was heavy. He had to drag it to the table.
tug	I tug on the door, but it will not open.

OPPOSITES: push, shove

push	I will push the wagon down the street.
poke	Don't poke your finger in your eye.
shove	Marie had to shove her brother out of the way of the car.

OPPOSITES: drag, pull, tug

put	Always put on clean clothes for school.
lay	The farmer will lay hay on the floor of the barn.
place	The teacher places books on the shelf.
set	Please set the roses on this table.

run

R

rain	The rain lasted all day.
shower	The sun was shining during the shower.
storm	The storm woke me up last night.

rope	The girl used a rope to tie the boat to the dock.
cord	Ted wrapped strong cord around the papers.
ribbon	The birthday present was tied with ribbon.
string	Mother used string to tie the tomato plants to the poles.
thread	Angela used a needle and thread to sew a button on her coat.

run	Carlos can run faster than anyone in class.
dash	Bob had to dash out of his house to catch the bus.
gallop	The wild horses gallop across the open land.
race	The three boys will race each other to see who is fastest.

OPPOSITES: crawl, step, tramp, walk

say	

S

say	I always say "thank you" when I get a present.
call	Please raise your hand when I call your name.
shout	Don't shout out the answer before I can say it.
speak	Speak clearly when you ask a question.
whisper	Whisper your secret in my ear.
see	Maureen will see the full moon in the evening sky.
gaze	Beth can gaze out the train window at the towns.
look	You should never look right at the sun.
peek	The baby likes to peek from behind the blankets.
peep	You can peep at the new baby while she sleeps.
stare	Sue had to stare at the big, flowery hat on the woman's head.
watch	My father and I like to watch football games.

	slide

shake	Shake this juice well before you drink it.
rattle	The strong winds rattle the windows.
rock	Grandmother likes to rock in her rocking chair.
shiver	The swimmers shiver when they get out of the pool.
shine	We see stars shine at night.
flash	Flash your light in this dark corner.
gleam	Clean windows gleam in the sunlight.
glow	A cat's eyes glow in the dark.
sparkle	The city lights sparkle at night.
twinkle	The plane's lights seem to twinkle like stars.
slide	Slide down the snowy hill on this sled.
coast	The wagon will coast to a stop at the bottom of the hill.
glide	The skaters glide over the smooth ice.
slip	The walk is icy. Be careful that you don't slip.

sound		throw

sound   The sound of traffic filled the city.

bang   The screen door slammed shut with a bang.

crash   There was a loud crash when Ted dropped the bowl.

roar   The lion's roar is very loud.

stop   We must stop doing our homework to have supper.

close   Bill will close his letter with "Yours truly."

finish   The workers will finish their job soon.

quit   The men quit work at 5:00 in the afternoon.

OPPOSITES: **begin, continue, start**

store   Charles bought his boots at this store.

market   We buy fresh foods at the market.

shop   Mandy's shop sells clothes for children.

story   Our teacher read the story aloud.

report   Jim wrote a report on dinosaurs.

tale   She told us a tale about a boy and his duck.

swim   Anne will swim from the boat to the shore.

paddle   My sister swims well. I can only paddle across the pool.

splash   The children splash in the pool.

teach   My father will teach me to ride a bicycle.

coach   Who will coach the football team this year?

show   Will you show her how to tie her shoes?

train   The girl can train the dog to catch a ball.

think   I think you should turn here.

believe   Do you believe the story?

wonder   I wonder who will win the game.

throw   Throw the stick and let the dog get it for us.

pitch   Maria will pitch the ball to the batter.

toss   The clowns toss the balls in the air.

OPPOSITE: **catch**

tie

tie	Climbers must tie ropes around their waists.
fasten	The captain asked us to fasten our seatbelts.
knot	First knot the ribbon, and then tie a bow.

OPPOSITES: loosen, untie

trap	Some people trap animals for food.
capture	We will capture a ladybug and let it go.
catch	The police have to catch the thief.

turn	Please turn around to see me.
spin	The children's pinwheels spin in the wind.
twist	Sally must twist in her seat to see the back of the room.
whirl	The dancer can whirl on one toe.
wind	Wind the end of the rope around the tree.

W

walk	We can walk to the beach, but Mel will drive us back.
crawl	The baby can crawl across the floor to his father.

way

cross	We cross the street at the light.
march	We like to march around the room to the music.
step	Step to the back of the room.

want	I want to help clean the house.
hope	The farmers hope the seeds will grow.
wish	I wish that every day could be Saturday.

wash	You should always wash fruit before you eat it.
clean	The man will clean the floor with soap and water.

way	Is this the way to the train station?
path	We have a brick path in front of our house.
road	The main road was blocked with cars.
street	Which house on this street is yours?
track	We ran around the track four times.
trail	The deer trail led into the woods.

WRITER'S GUIDE

SPELLING RULES

Unit 1: **Beginning Sounds**

Every letter is a consonant except <u>a</u>, <u>e</u>, <u>i</u>, <u>o</u>, <u>u</u>, and sometimes <u>y</u>. The first letter in each of these words is a consonant.

- **b** as in <u>band</u>
- **m** as in <u>men</u>
- **n** as in <u>next</u>
- **p** as in <u>pan</u>
- **r** as in <u>rest</u>

Unit 2: **Beginning Sounds**

Here are consonant letters that begin words.

- **t** as in <u>tell</u>
- **d** as in <u>dear</u>
- **f** as in <u>fit</u>
- **v** as in <u>very</u>
- **w** as in <u>went</u>
- **y** as in <u>your</u>

Unit 3: **Beginning Sounds**

Here are consonant letters that begin words.

- **g** as in <u>gold</u>
- **h** as in <u>hall</u>
- **j** as in <u>jet</u>
- **l** as in <u>left</u>
- **s** as in <u>soon</u>

Unit 4: **The Sound /k/**

Here are three ways to spell /k/.

- with **c**, as in <u>cup</u>
- with **k**, as in <u>kite</u>
- with **ck**, as in <u>duck</u>

Unit 5: **Spelling Short a̲**

- This is the sign for short a̲: /a/. You spell the vowel sound /a/ with the letter **a** as in these words.

  ant   fast   hand

Unit 7: **Spelling Short e̲**

- This is the sign for short e̲: /e/. You spell the vowel sound /e/ with the letter **e** as in these words.

  pet   dress   well

Unit 8: **Spelling Short i̲**

- This is the sign for short i̲: /i/. You spell the vowel sound /i/ with the letter **i** as in these words.

  fill   hit   is

Unit 9: **Spelling Short u̲**

- This is the sign for short u̲: /u/. Most of the time, you spell the vowel sound /u/ with the letter **u** as in these words.

  until   truck   jump

- ☐ The sound /u/ can also be spelled with the letter **o** as in the words below. Each of these words also ends with an e̲.

  come   done   some

Unit 10: **Words with o**

- This is the sign for short o: /o/. You spell the vowel sound /o/ with the letter **o** as in these words.

    top   pond   shop

- ☐ The vowel sound you hear in dog is /ô/. This vowel sound is also spelled with the letter **o.**

Unit 11: **Double Letters**

Some words end with a consonant sound that is spelled with two letters that are alike. We call these letters **double consonant letters.**

- **zz** as in buzz
- **ss** as in miss
- **ll** as in fell
- **gg** as in egg
- **ff** as in off

Unit 13: **Consonant Clusters**

A **consonant cluster** is made up of consonant letters that you write together. You hear the sounds of the letters together as in these words.

- **st** as in stand and most
- **gl** as in glad
- **pl** as in place

Unit 14: **Consonant Clusters**

Here are consonant clusters.

- **sm** as in <u>small</u>
- **sp** as in <u>spot</u>
- **sw** as in <u>swim</u>
- **br** as in <u>brother</u>
- **fr** as in <u>from</u>
- **gr** as in <u>great</u>
- **pr** as in <u>pretty</u>
- **tr** as in <u>true</u>

Unit 15: **The Letters <u>sh</u> and <u>th</u>**

- The two letters **sh** may stand for one consonant sound.
  sheep   shoe   dish

- The two letters **th** may stand for one consonant sound.
  thank   thing   teeth

Unit 16: **The Letters <u>th</u> and <u>ch</u>**

- The two letters **th** may stand for one consonant sound.
  their   them   these

- The two letters **ch** may stand for one consonant sound.
  chair   each   lunch

- ☐ In <u>watch</u>, the sound that **ch** stands for is spelled with three letters: **tch**.

Unit 17: **Words to Remember**

- The letters **ere** may stand for different sounds.
  there   here   were

Unit 19: **Spelling Long <u>a</u>**

* This is the sign for long <u>a</u>: /ā/. You can spell /ā/ with **a**-consonant-**e** as in these words.

  > ate   gave   same

Unit 20: **More Ways to Spell /ā/**

Here are three ways to spell /ā/.

* with **ai** in the middle of words, as in <u>plain</u>
* with **ay** at the end of words, as in <u>may</u>
* □ with **ey**, as at the end of <u>they</u>

Unit 21: **Spelling Long <u>e</u>**

This is the sign for long <u>e</u>: /ē/. Here are three ways to spell /ē/.

* with **ee,** as in <u>free</u>
* with **ea,** as in leave
* with **y,** as in <u>many</u>

Unit 22: **Spelling Long <u>i</u>**

* This is the sign for long <u>i</u>: /ī/. You can spell /ī/ with **i**-consonant-**e** as in these words.

  > bike   side   tire

* □ The word <u>give</u> doesn't have the sound /ī/. But it is spelled with **i**-consonant-**e**.

Unit 23: **More Ways to Spell /ī/**

Here are four ways to spell /ī/.

- with **y** at the end of a word, as in <u>dry</u>
- with **i** before **nd**, as in <u>kind</u>
- with **igh** as in <u>high</u>
- ☐ with **ie** at the end of a word, as in <u>tie</u>

Unit 25: **Spelling Long <u>o</u>**

This is the sign for long <u>o</u>: /ō/. Here are two ways to spell /ō/.

- with **o**-consonant-**e** as in <u>note</u>
- with **ow** as in <u>low</u>

Unit 26: **More Ways to Spell /ō/**

Here are two ways to spell /ō/.

- with **o,** as in <u>told</u>
- with **oa,** as in <u>soap</u>

Unit 27: **Words with <u>ng</u> and <u>nk</u>**

- The two letters **ng** stand for one sound.
  - long   hang   young

- The **ng** in <u>long</u> and the **n** in <u>trunk</u> stand for the same sound.
  You hear that sound in <u>trunk</u> just before /k/.
  - trunk   bank   drink

► *WRITER'S GUIDE*

Unit 28: **The Sound /o͞o/ in boot**

This is the sign for the vowel sound in boot: /o͞o/. Here are three ways to spell /o͞o/.

- with one **o,** as in two
- with **oo,** as in boot
- with **ew,** as in blew

Unit 29: **The Sound /o͝o/ in pull**

This is the sign for the vowel sound in pull: /o͝o/. Here are three ways to spell /o͝o/.

- with **u,** as in pull
- with **oo,** as in foot
- with **ou,** as in could

Unit 31: **The Sound /ô/ in paw**

This is the sign for the vowel sound in paw: /ô/. Here are three ways to spell /ô/.

- with **a,** as in fall
- with **aw,** as in paw
- with **au,** as in because

Unit 32: **The Sound /ou/ in out**

This is the sign for the vowel sound in out: /ou/. Here are two ways to spell /ou/.

- with **ou,** as in out
- with **ow,** as in tower

Unit 33: **Vowel Sounds with r**

Some words have a vowel sound followed by r. This is the sign for the vowel sound followed by r in part: /är/. This is the sign for the vowel sound followed by r in torn: /ôr/. Here are three ways to spell the vowel sound /ôr/.

- with **or** as in <u>torn</u>
- with **ore** as in <u>more</u>
- ☐ with **oor** as in <u>door</u>

Unit 34: **Vowel Sounds with r**

This is the sign for the vowel sound followed by r in <u>near</u>: /ir/. Here is one way to spell the vowel sound /ir/.

- with **ear** as in <u>hear</u>

This is the sign for the vowel sound followed by r in <u>her</u>: /ûr/. Here are four ways to spell /ûr/.

- with **er,** as in <u>her</u>
- with **ir,** as in <u>girl</u>
- with **or,** as in <u>word</u>
- with **ur,** as in <u>turn</u>

Unit 35: **The Sounds /ər/**

Some words end with a weak vowel sound and r. The weak vowel sound is called **schwa**. This is the sign for schwa: /ə/. Here are three ways to spell /ər/.

- with **er,** as in <u>winter</u>
- with **or,** as in <u>color</u>
- with **ar,** as in <u>dollar</u>

TROUBLESOME WORDS TO SPELL

always	friend	mother	teacher
am	from	Mrs.	Thanksgiving
and	fun	much	that's
aunt	good	name	their
baby	had	nice	there
balloon	Halloween	now	time
because	has	on	to
bought	have	once	today
boy	he	one	tomorrow
brother	here	our	too
brought	him	party	train
can	his	people	two
children	house	play	very
cousin	I'm	pretty	we
didn't	in	said	were
dog	know	saw	white
don't	little	snow	write
everybody	made	some	writing
father	make	sometimes	you
for	me	store	your

LANGUAGE: A Glossary of Words and Examples

Grammar

Sentences

- A **sentence** is a group of words that tells a complete thought. Every sentence begins with a **capital letter**.
    The balloon is red.

- A **statement** tells something. It ends with a period (.).
    Pablo walked to the store.

- A **question** asks something. It ends with a question mark(**?**).
    Is that a new dress?

Nouns

- A noun is a word that names a person, place, or thing.
    letter   house   sister

- Add **s** to most nouns to mean more than one.
    school—schools   apple—apples
    friend—friends   car—cars

- Add **es** to most nouns that end in **x**, **ch**, **sh**, or **s** to mean more than one.
    box—boxes   lunch—lunches
    dish—dishes   glass—glasses

Verbs

- An **action verb** is a word that shows an action.
    write   eat   drop   swim

- Add **s** to an action verb that tells about one person or thing.
    One cat jumps.   Three cats jump.

- Verbs can tell about action in the past. Form the past time of most verbs by adding **ed**.
    Today I paint.   Yesterday I painted.

- Some action verbs do not add **ed** to tell about the past.

Present	Past
go, goes	went
feel, feels	felt
run, runs	ran
tell, tells	told

- Some verbs do not show action.

Present	Past
am, is, are	was, were
have, has	had

Describing Words

- A **describing word** is a word that describes a noun.
    I saw a funny movie.

- Add **er** to most describing words when they are used to compare two things.
    A horse is taller than a dog.

- Add **est** to most describing words when they are used to compare more than two things.
    That is the tallest tree in the forest.

Vocabulary

Opposites

- Some words have opposite meanings.

  shut—open   same—different
  little—big   top—bottom

Compound Words

- A **compound word** is made up of two smaller words.

  afternoon   inside   someone

Words That Sound the Same

- The words **to, too**, and **two** sound alike but are spelled differently.

- **To** helps to tell where. **To** can also come before a verb.

  Are you going <u>to</u> the lake?
  I want <u>to</u> go with you.

- **Too** means "also" or "more than enough."

  She won a prize, <u>too</u>.
  He put <u>too</u> much salt in the soup.

- **Two** is the word for the numeral <u>2</u>.

  I saw <u>two</u> raccoons in the yard.

Rhyming Words

- **Rhyming words** are words that end with the same sounds.

  flower—tower   free—three
  shoe—blew   fun—sun

DICTIONARY: A Glossary of Words and Examples

ABC Order

- The order of letters from A to Z is called ABC order. Words in a dictionary are in ABC order. These words are in ABC order.

ball

dog

how

town

well

Guide Words

- The two words at the top of a dictionary page are called **guide words**. The word on the left is the first word on the page. The word on the right is the last word on the page. All the other words on the page are in ABC order between the first and last word.

along	be

along　We followed the path along the edge of the cliff. My dog came along with us.

also　Brian plays the piano. He also plays the drums.

asleep　Kevin was so tired, he fell asleep in the chair.

at　I met Ralph at the zoo. We had fun looking at the animals.

Entry Word

- An **entry word** is a word that is in **dark print** on a dictionary page. Entry words are in ABC order.
- Some entry words have more than one meaning.
- The dictionary shows how to use entry words in sentences.

---

order **1** Put the words in ABC order. **2** The captain gave the order to march.

other I found one shoe, but I can't find the other one.

our My sister and I made a cake for our mother's birthday.

COMPOSITION

Guides for Writing

Before Writing

Use this checklist to plan your writing.

- Think about what you want to write.
- Think about why you are writing.
- Think about who will read your work.
- Ask yourself questions about your idea.
- Make a plan.
- Read over your plan.
- Add more ideas to your plan as you think of them.

Here are some ways you can plan what you write.

LISTMAKING
Thinking of Words

Parade

bands	flags	balloons
clowns	music	jugglers
singing	animals	clapping

CLUSTERING
Planning Sentences

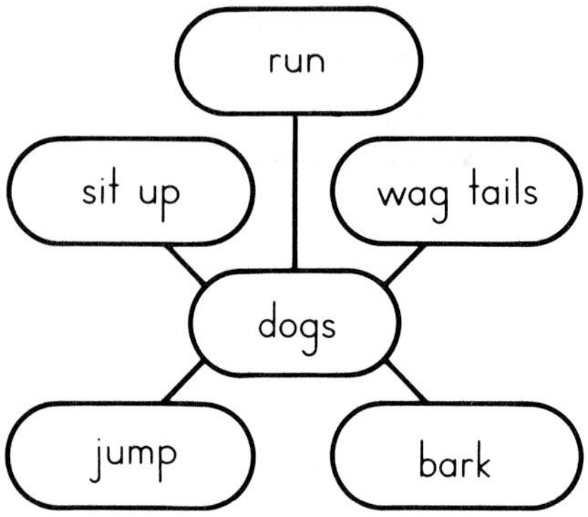

run

sit up   wag tails

dogs

jump   bark

CHARTING
Sensory Details

<u>S</u>ee	<u>H</u>ear	<u>T</u>aste	<u>F</u>eel	<u>S</u>mell
beach	waves crashing	salty water	hot sand	fresh air
picnic	people talking	sour lemonade	cool grass	meat cooking

MAPPING
Drawing a Plan

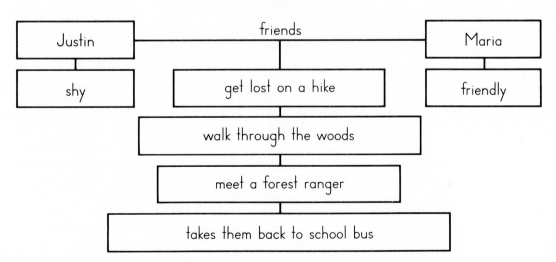

Writing

Use this checklist as you write.

- Read over your plan.
- Use your plan.
- Write quickly.
- Do not worry about mistakes.
- Remember that you may get more ideas.
- Add any new ideas as you think of them.
- Think about why you are writing.
- Think about who will read what you write.

After Writing

Use this checklist when you edit and proofread your work.

Editing

- Read over your work.
- Be sure the statements tell something.
- Check that each sentence gives a complete thought.
- Be sure the questions ask something.
- Be sure each paragraph has a clear topic sentence.
- Check that all the detail sentences support the main idea.
- Be sure the words are lively and interesting.

Proofreading

- Be sure every sentence begins with a capital letter.
- Be sure you used periods and question marks correctly.
- Check the spelling of each word.
- Be sure the first line of each paragraph is indented.
- Be sure your handwriting is neat and readable.

Editing and Proofreading Marks

- Use Editing and Proofreading Marks when you revise your writing. These marks help you see the changes you want to make.
- Remember that you can change words and sentences as many times as you want to.

all students are going to the school fair It will
writing ⊙
be next Tuesday. There will be a ∧ contest and an art

show. The fair will be on May 11 ∧ 19--. Teachers
Prizes
and families and pets are invited. Prises will be

given for the best writing. ¶ The fair is always fun.

Everyone is working to make this fair the best ever.

Editing and Proofreading Marks

≡	capitalize
⊙	make a period
∧	add something
℘	take something away
∧,	add a comma
◯	spell correctly
¶	indent the paragraph

A Glossary of Words and Examples

Kinds of Sentences

- A **sentence** is a group of words that tells a complete thought. Every sentence begins with a capital letter.
  The balloon is red.

- A **statement** tells something. It ends with a period (.).
  Pablo walked to the store.

- A **question** asks something. It ends with a question mark (**?**).
  Is that a new dress?

Paragraph

- A **paragraph** is a group of sentences that tell about one main idea.
- The first line of a paragraph is indented.

Here is an example of a paragraph.

> Katie is a good swimmer. She swims in the pool every day. She swims to the end of the pool and back. Katie thinks swimming is fun.

Paragraph that Describes

- A **paragraph that describes** makes a picture with words. It tells how something <u>looks</u>, <u>feels</u>, <u>sounds</u>, <u>tastes</u> or <u>smells</u>.

Here is an example of a paragraph that describes.

> A squirrel visited our yard last week. Its fur was thick and gray. It had tiny black paws and a bushy tail. Sometimes the squirrel was as still as a stone. Then it would run quickly away.

How-to Paragraph

- A **how-to paragraph** tells how to do something.
- The first sentence tells what the paragraph is about.
- The next sentences tell how to do something in order.
- How-to paragraphs use the words <u>first</u>, <u>next</u>, <u>then</u>, and <u>last</u> to show the order of steps.

Here is an example of a how-to paragraph.

> This is how I give my dog Rokko a bath. First I fill the bathtub with water. I put Rokko in the bathtub. Next I wash Rokko's fur with soap and water. Then I rinse it with a hose. Last I dry Rokko with a towel.

Friendly Letter

- A **friendly letter** is a letter you write to someone you know.
- A friendly letter has five parts.
- The **heading** gives the date you wrote the letter. Use a **comma (,)** between the day and the year in the heading.
- The **greeting** says hello to the person to whom you are writing. Use a **comma (,)** after the greeting.
- The **body** is the part in which you write your message.
- The **closing** ends the letter. Use a **comma (,)** after the closing.
- The **signature** is your name signed by yourself.

An example of a friendly letter is on the next page.

Here is an example of a friendly letter.

May 11, 19--	**Heading**
Dear Penny,	**Greeting**
I have a new puppy. I named it Spikey. Spikey sleeps in a box near the stove. Please visit me soon.	**Body**
Love,	**Closing**
Adam	**Signature**

List

- A **list** helps people to remember things or to put things in order.

Here is an example of a list.

Things To Do

clean my room

polish my shoes

write Grandma

do my homework

Note

- A **note** is a short message.

Here is an example of a note.

Bob,

Dave called. Please call him.

Jane

Story

- A **story** has a beginning, a middle, and an ending.
- The **beginning** tells whom the story is about. It also tells where the story takes place.
- The **middle** tells what happens first and what happens next in the story.
- The **ending** tells how everything in the story turns out.
- A story has a title.

Here is an example of a story.

Jimmy Goes Fishing

Jimmy went to the beach. He wanted to catch a fish for dinner. First he tied some bait to the string. Then he sat on the dock and put the string in the water. Soon a fish bit the bait. Jimmy smiled. Then he pulled up the fish and put it in his pail. That night, Jimmy had fresh fish for dinner.

Two-Line Rhyme

- A **two-line rhyme** is a rhyme in which each line ends with a rhyming word.

Here is an example of a two-line rhyme.

Rain, rain, go away.
Come again another day.

Poem

- A **poem** can paint a picture with words.
- A poem can help you to see something in a new way.
- Some poems use **rhyming words**.

Here is an example of a poem.

> From my window I can see
> Sunlight dancing in a tree.
> It warms away the winter cold,
> And turns the leaves to summer gold.

MECHANICS: A Glossary of Rules

Capital Letters

Names and Titles of Persons and <u>I</u>

- Begin the name of a person with a capital letter.
  Don Bracken   Maria Lopez

- Begin titles of people with capital letters. Put a period after <u>Ms.</u>, <u>Mrs.</u>, <u>Mr.</u>, and <u>Dr</u>.

- Always write the word <u>I</u> with a capital letter.

Names of Places

- Begin the names of streets with capital letters.
  61 Clinton Avenue

- Begin the names of cities and states with capital letters.
  Houston, Texas   Portland, Maine

Capital Letters

Names of Days, Months, and Holidays

- Begin the name of a day of the week with a capital letter.
  Monday   Wednesday   Saturday

- Begin the name of a month with a capital letter.
  March   June   September

Names of Books and Stories

- Begin the first word, last word, and all important words in a title with a capital letter.
  <u>A Funny Surprise</u>   <u>The Cat in a Tree</u>

Punctuation

Period

- Use a period (.) at the end of a statement.
  I have a pet rabbit.

Question Mark

- Use a question mark (?) at the end of a question.
  Where are you going?

Comma

- Use a comma (,) between the name of a city and a state.
  Mesa, Arizona   Lexington, Virginia

- Use a comma (,) between the day and the year in a date.
  September 8, 1954

HANDWRITING: Alphabet and Common Errors

Uppercase Manuscript Alphabet

Lowercase Manuscript Alphabet

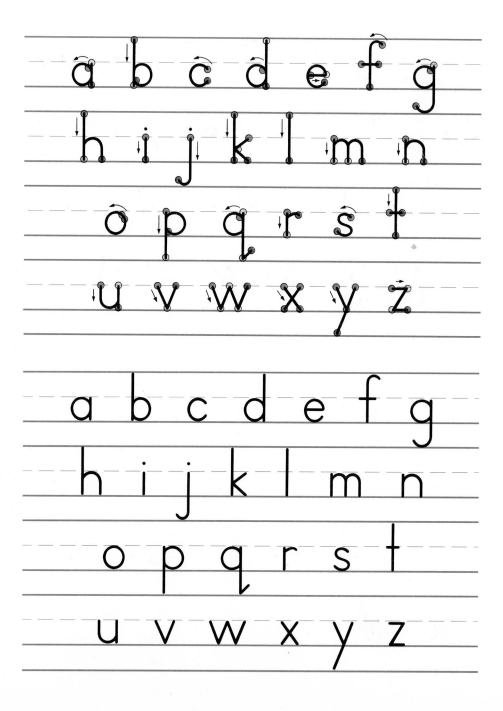

Uppercase Cursive Alphabet

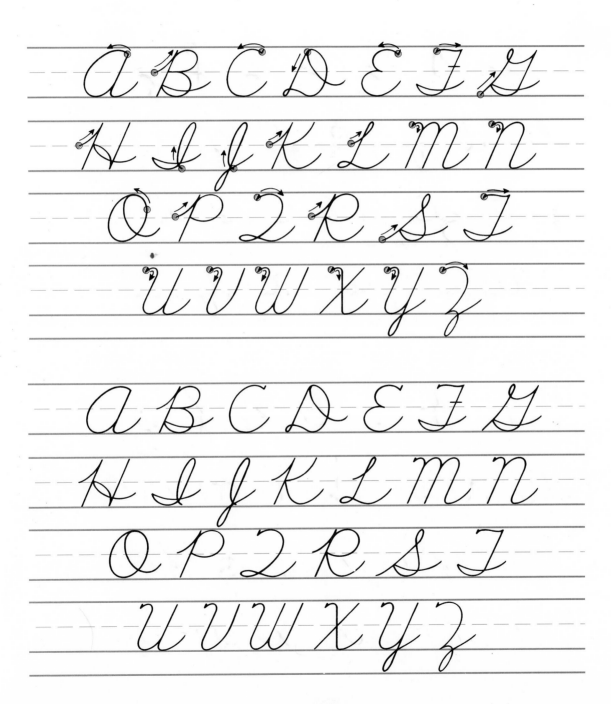

Lowercase Cursive Alphabet

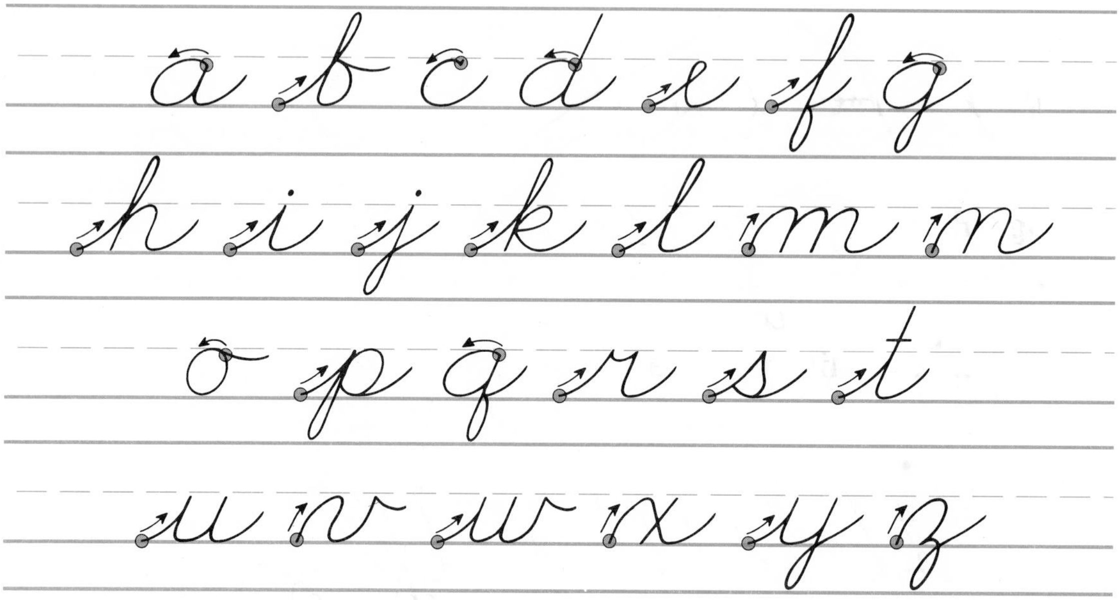

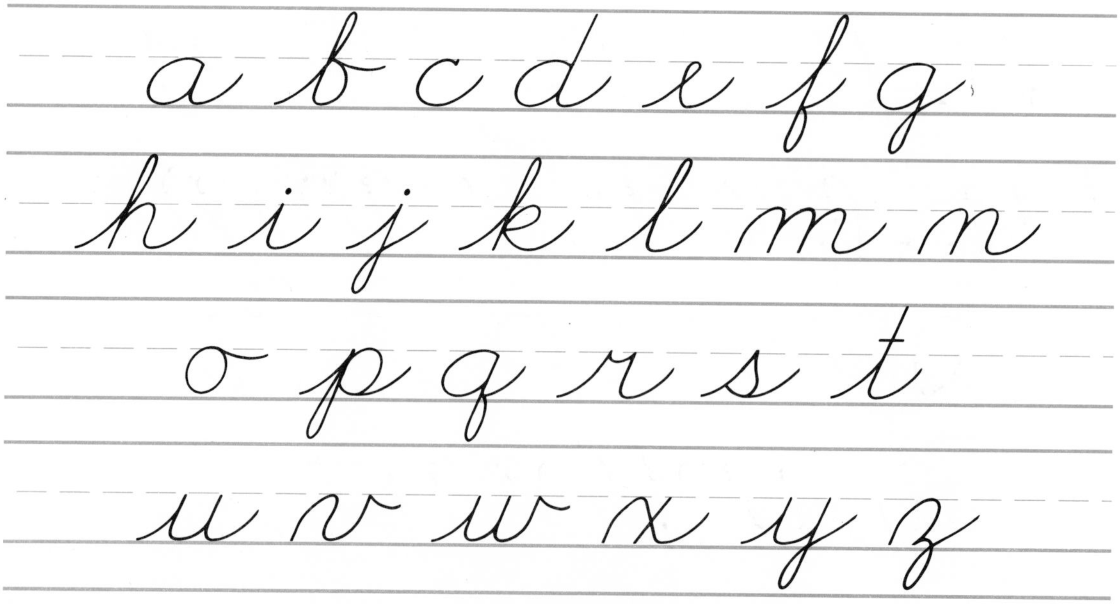

a b c d e f g
h i j k l m n
o p q r s t
u v w x y z

a b c d e f g
h i j k l m n
o p q r s t
u v w x y z

Common Errors–Manuscript Letters

- Write the letters correctly.

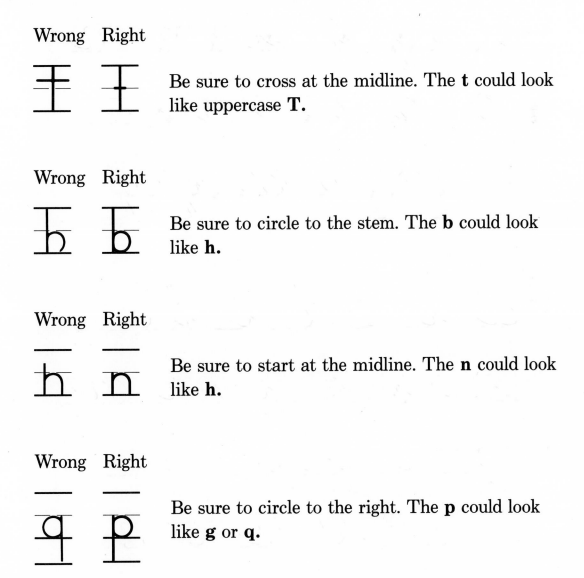

Wrong Right

Be sure to cross at the midline. The **t** could look like uppercase **T**.

Wrong Right

Be sure to circle to the stem. The **b** could look like **h**.

Wrong Right

Be sure to start at the midline. The **n** could look like **h**.

Wrong Right

Be sure to circle to the right. The **p** could look like **g** or **q**.

WRITER'S GUIDE

- Write the letters correctly.

Wrong   Right

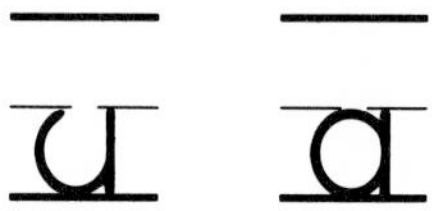

Be sure to start slightly below the midline.
The **a** could look like **u.**

Wrong   Right

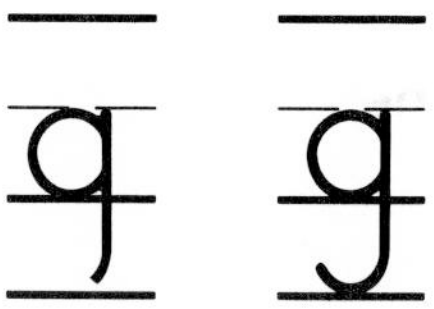

Be sure to curve the tail stroke to the left.
The **g** could look like **q.**

Wrong   Right

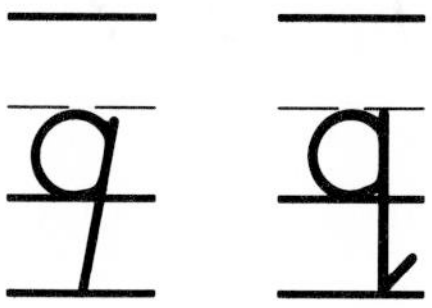

Be sure to make the slant stroke. The **q** could
look like **g.**

Wrong   Right

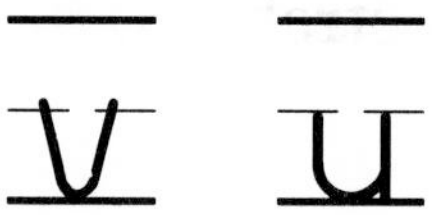

Be sure to retrace to the bottom line. The **u**
could look like **v.**

• Write the letters correctly.

Wrong   Right

Be sure to slant the first stroke.
The **v** could look like **r**.

Wrong   Right

Be sure to go straight across to the right. The **z** could look like **s**.

Wrong   Right

Be sure to start at the midline. The **y** could look like uppercase **Y**.

Wrong   Right

Be sure to use the straight across strokes. The **I** could look like lowercase **l**.

• Write the letters correctly.

Wrong   Right

    Be sure the strokes go straight down.
The **H** could look like **A.**

Wrong   Right

    Be sure to close the circle. The **O** could look
like **C.**

Wrong   Right

    Be sure to use the straight across stroke.
The **G** could look like **C.**

Wrong   Right

Be sure to use straight slant strokes. The **V**
could look like **U.**

• Write the letters correctly.

Wrong   Right

Be sure to circle to the right and close.
The **B** could look like **R.**

Wrong   Right

Be sure to use a straight slant stroke.
The **K** could look like **R.**

Common Errors–Cursive Letters

⊙ Write the letters correctly.

Wrong   Right

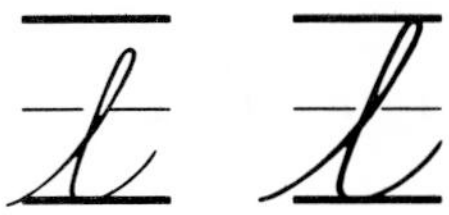

Be sure to loop to the top line. The **l** could look like **e.**

Wrong   Right

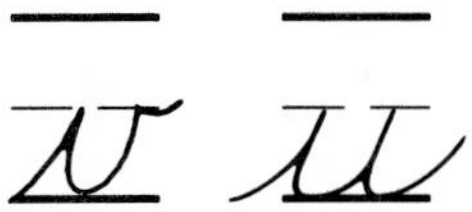

Be sure the slant stroke returns to the bottom line. The **u** could look like **v.**

Wrong   Right

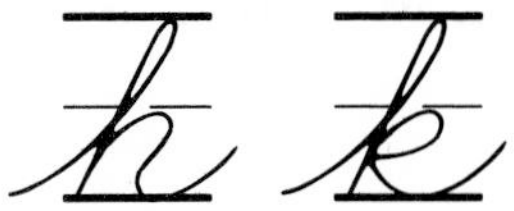

Be sure to touch the stem. The **k** could look like **h.**

Wrong   Right

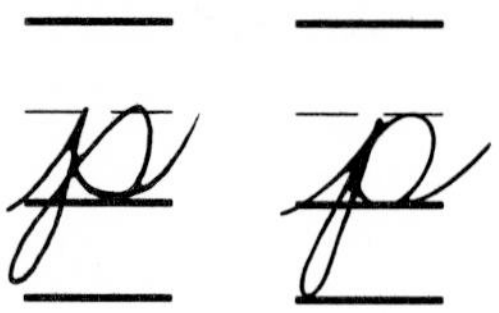

Be sure to loop the bottom line. The **p** could look like **js.**

• Write the letters correctly.

Wrong   Right

Be sure to make a long joining stroke. The **ra** could look like **rc.**

Wrong   Right

Be sure to close the **o.** The **o** could look like **c.**

Wrong   Right

Be sure to loop left. The **g** could look like **q.**

Wrong   Right

Be sure to use only two up-and-over strokes. The **n** could look like **m.**

267

• Write the letters correctly.

Wrong   Right

Be sure to see **v** before joining the next letter. The **ve** could look like **re**.

Wrong   Right

Be sure not to join **P** to other letters. The **P** could look like **R**.

Wrong   Right

Be sure to make only one overcurve. The **N** could look like **M**.

Wrong   Right

Be sure to retrace for the joining stroke. The **U** could look like **V**.

• Write the letters correctly.

Wrong Right

 Be sure to cross **F**. The **F** could look like **T**.

Wrong Right

 Be sure to close the **A** and use a straight retrace stroke. The **A** could look like **Cl**.

Wrong Right

 Be sure to start at the midline and undercurve to the top line. The **L** could look like **Q**.

Wrong Right

 Be sure to slant to the top line. The **S** could look like lowercase **s**.

Wrong Right

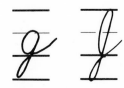 Be sure to start at the bottom line and curve up to the left. The **J** could look like lowercase **g**.

8
9
0
E 1
F 2
G 3
H 4
I 5
J 6